BLOBS!

BOOK OF

LIMERICKS,

ODES, BALLADS

AND SONNETS

IN THE LIGHTER MOOD

STANLEY HEMMING-CLARK

B L O B S

BOOK OF LIMERICKS, ODES, BALLADS AND SONNETS IN THE LIGHTER MOOD

Themes include:
Men and Women
Natural and Unnatural World
Misunderstandings
Food
Training the Young
The Classical World
Holy Laughter
and various other bits

© Searchline Publishing 2022
First edition 2022

ISBN: 978 1 897864 67 8
British Library Cataloguing in Publication Data available
Published by Searchline Publishing, Searchline House,
Holbrook Lane, Chislehurst, Kent, BR7 6PE, UK

Tel & Fax: 020 8468 7945
www.johnhemmingclark.com/stanleyhemmingclark

Printed in England by: www.catfordprint.co.uk

About the author: Stanley Hemming-Clark was born in
1929. He read Latin with French, and Theology at
Cambridge. He was vicar of a Kent village for thirty-eight
years, at times combining this with the chaplaincy of a
convalescent home and a teaching post. He now lives near
Guilford. He officiates in local churches when needed and
teaches Latin to U3A members.

Drawings by the author.

By the same author

Unity, Uniformity and the English Church
A R Mowbray 1961

The Second Advent
A R Mowbray 1963

Hymns and Meditations on the Seven Words from the Cross
Searchlne Publishing 1999

It's a Cat's Life
Searchline Publishing 2009

If Memory be Truth
Searchline Publishing 2017

www.johnhemmingclark.com/stanleyhemmingclark
Facebook: @stanleyhemmingclark

Contents

Foreword by the Author

"Tenet insanabile multos scribendi cacoethes, et aegro in corde senescit" wrote Juvenal. (The crazy urge to write grips many, and grows old in a sick heart).

I have certainly grown old writing comic verse since I am ninety-three years old and have been doing it for seventy-five years. At school my parody of Chaucer's Prologue, describing some of the staff, annoyed the French master, who thought it was impertinent and maybe aegro corde until the headmaster said that it was very funny. At a college reunion a contemporary remarked, "I only remember two things about you - you could not sing in tune and wrote comic verse." In a recent history of my theological college, amid the great and the good, leading bishops and so on, I get one mention - for writing the lyrics of a comic opera. In thirty-eight years as an incumbent this habit has both amused parishioners and at times defused difficult situations.

Of course, much is of interest only to those particular individuals or events, but those here may amuse a wider group. I offer them as the insanabile products of a senex, but not I hope aegro corde. Others may have different opinions. Some are based on jokes heard, for which I give thanks.

The first one had a prize in the Folio Society's competition and was published in the summer 1995 edition of Folio. Characters from Chaucer's Prologue appear in The London Marathone.

Stanley Hemming-Clark

1

The London Marathonne

Whan that Aprille with his shoures sote
Inspired the crowds to line the London route
And stonden alle daie in yonge sonne,
Than longen folk to run in Marathonne.
To Blackheath they cam from east and weste,
Everychon had nombre on hir veste,
Or sponsor's name on hir queyntise;
For guerdone they ran, as I now devyse.

A gentil KNYGHT ther was, a worthy Name,
But colerik, to tellen of his shame:
He ran for goodes and for his estate,
Alle lost at Lloydes by cruelle fate.
With him a SQUYER, fresh as the month of Maie,
Yet burdened with a heavy debt to paie:
To train as Squyer, he told us with a groan,
His Graunt hadde ben y-changed to a Loan.
A povre PERSOUN, his flock for to feed,
And bild his chirche, did money need:
This holy manne wept much and told
How Chirche Commissioners hadde lost hir gold.
With him a LADY PRESTE did flirte,
Amor Vincit Omnia on hir T-shirte;
For holy bookes she ranne, that folks might read,
Alle pur, from sexist wordes freed.
A PLOWMAN ther was, a wight of hevy build;
He was y-sponsored by the Plowmannes Guild;
No cash they hadde; ne swynk at Harvest tide;
Ne sow ne repe; hir Lond was Sette A Side.
A SHIPMAN ther was, who ledde daie trippes,
Now povre and neding Sponsors for his shippes;
A tunnel was y-dugge; men need not sale,
Beneath the seas they feared ne Wind ne Gale.
A WYF OF BATH full deintly did hoppe
With many goodes from out the Bodye Shoppe;
She only ranne - so sedde some evil wight -
For slyming sake, to make hir hippes light.

I watched alle runne; then took up my pen,
These words to write, than reade on News atte Tenn.

2

Men and Women

This first section, pages 3 to 27, begins appropriately with thoughts at a wedding, but shows how these thoughts are signs of old age.

This reflects the Introduction *aegro in corde senescit* - grows old in a sick heart.

Confessions by (not to) a Vicar
The sign that I am growing old,
I must confess, if truth be told -
When at weddings I officiate
And there with young folk celebrate,
As the Wedding Group I see,
The Bride's Mother seems to me
More attractive than her daughter.
(Which a vicar did not oughter!)

We now pass to three ballads about young men desperate for love.

The Ballad of the Lonely Heart
Thoughts on reading the singles pages of the local newspaper.

Young Reginald lived in his flat alone;
He was shy (though his thoughts were bold).
His secret wish was a girl of his own,
Whom his manly arms might enfold.

Yet neither at work and nor at play
Did he meet Miss Right, though he yearned;
Until at last in his paper one day
To the LONELY HEARTS section he turned.

Details were there in three or four pages
And many sad stories they showed:
Ladies all colours, sizes and ages,
And some had strange letters in code.

First then he chose: "Young widow of forty,
Slim, outdoor sports," (Needs a new mate!)
"G.S.O.H." (Could that code be naughty...?)
So he rang and made a first date.

Their meal was now over... time to be bold!
"Come off for a week as my wife."
"No! No!" she replied, "Though jokes I have told,
You don't laugh - so not on your life!"

"Great Sex On Holiday - you surely meant -
Mad love and passion desired."
"You fool," she replied, "Your mind must be bent -
It's Good Sense Of Humour required."

His second attempt was: "Brunette, petite,
Shy, lonely, and needs T.L.C."
I see what she needs, so soon as we meet
Tough, Lustful and Crafty I'll be!

He grabbed the shy girl and bit her soft ear,
His grip like a big grizzly bear.
She struggled and screamed, "You've a strange idea
of Tender and Loving and Care!"

His third was: "Well-built lady of fifty."
"W.L.T.M." was her sign.
"Cycling and walking: tastes are quite thrifty."
Thought Reginald: "She'd suit me fine."

"T is for Tender - that one I can tell;
M is for Man - clear as can be.
W must be Winsome and Lovely is L;
Winsome, lovely, tender man - me!"

With simpering smile and best aftershave,
He took roses smelling so sweet.
She, slapping his back, said with farewell wave:
"You're not the one I Would Like To Meet!"

Next on his list: "Girl, single, just thirty:
Some L.T.R. would suit me best:
I'm a honey blond, fluffy and flirty."
"Learned, Thoughtful, Reader," he guessed.

Specs thick and black he made assignation
With Wittgenstein under his arms.
"Stuff your books! A Long-Term Relation-
Ship's the price," she said, "for my charms."

Envoi
Our hero sat on his own in despair:
Sadly he turned over the page -
And saw an advert: "Man want to share
ADULT GAMES, no matter what age."

"No letters in code; no reason to doubt:
What they want is clear as the day
I won't get this wrong," so our hero set out -
His Scrabble set ready to play...!

The Metamorphosis or Transformation of Norman

In nova fert animus mutatas dicere formas corpora
Ovid. Metamorphoses 1:1
My mind is set to tell of bodies changed into new forms

To Norman fate had not been kind:
He led a lonely life.
Although he longed, he could not find
A lady for his wife.

He did not have a handsome face.
He had no wealth or gold.
He lacked all kind of social grace:
All witty words and bold.

One day he watched th' incoming tide
While sitting by the sea,
When all at once his eye espied
A bottle floating free.

"That may be something rare," thought he,
"Which I can sell or save."
So Norman walked into the sea
And plucked it from the wave.

He thought, "It's got some bits of dirt.
I don't know where it's been."
He used the tail end of his shirt
To wipe the bottle clean.

He wiped the bottle clean and bright
And then undid the top.
Much to our Norman's great surprise
A genie out did pop.

The genie said, "I promise you -
Three wishes you may say.
And all these wishes will come true.
Speak, master. I obey."

Our Norman cried, "O what a treat!
Some money would be fine,
Then I can have good food to eat
And take some girls to dine."

The genie waved his wand around
And spoke the magic spell.
Five million pounds our Norman found
In notes, with gold as well.

Then Norman said, "Thanks genie dear
For all that lovely cash.
My next wish - make a car appear
So I can cut a dash."

Once more the genie waved his wand
And suddenly he made
A motor worthy of James Bond,
Tax and insurance paid.

"I'm not a handsome man," said Norm,
"The third wish on my list -
Can I be changed into a form
No woman can resist."

Envoi
The genie, faithful to his name,
Gave with his wand three knocks,
And ugly Norman then became
A lovely chocolate box!

Ronald's Dilemma
A ballad

Young Ronald was an 'andsome lad
Of Cockney family.
Two pretty girls 'e loved like mad,
A puzzled lad was 'e.

Maria was quite tall and slim,
Brighter than most girls.
'Er thoughtful words delighted 'im.
'E loved 'er dark brown curls.

Sue was different, plump and round,
A fluffy blonde was Sue.
'E loved 'er laugh with merry sound,
And eyes of sparkling blue.

Now Ronald was a serious lad.
"You ought," said mum, "To wed."
But 'e could not make up 'is mind.
"Which shall I 'ave?" 'e said.

"'Tis vital I should choose aright,"
Said Ron with doubting mind.
'E felt that if 'e prayed aright,
Some guidance 'e would find.

At last to church Ron made 'is way
And by a statue knelt.
'E closed 'is eyes, began to pray
About the doubts 'e felt.

Envoi
Opening 'is eyes 'e raised 'is 'ead.
At last an answer clear!
Inscribed in shining gold 'e read
Two words - Ave Maria.

At last we come to an actual wedding. However well planned these are, something can always go wrong.

The Wedding Procession
An ode

When the bride processed up the church aisle to meet
Her groom at the altar there waiting,
She wore high-heeled shoes on her dainty fair feet.
One stuck in a hole in the grating.

With one dainty foot bare, continued the bride.
With commendable presence of mind,
Verger pulled out this grating - shoe stuck inside -
Which he solemnly carried behind.

Where the grating had been yawned a hole deep and wide
Which led down to the boiler below.
The vicar followed the verger and bride.
Alas! Into this hole he did go.

A happy marriage means that each partner should know the likes and preferences of the other. These two poems about young married couples explore this theme.

Cat Love

Friend to husband
> "You look a mess, my poor old friend,
> Cuts on your face, scratch on your ear,
> Bruise on your neck, pain when you bend.
> You've had an accident, I fear."

Husband
> "My wife, whom I dearly treasure,
> Has made me this painful sight.
> Making love, she gets her pleasure
> Pretending we're cats in the night."

Friend
> "I see, so in catlike fashion
> She gave you a scratch and a bite.
> In the mad heat of her passion
> She made you this painful sight."

Husband
> "My wounds weren't caused quite like that.
> In dark of night - this part is truth -
> We made love like a pussycat.
> But then I fell down from the roof."

The Early Morning Cuppa

When the young vicar and his wife, newly wed,
Still sleepy, awoke in the morning,
After their first night together in bed,
She said, as she stifled her yawning -

"My love, there's one little thing I must ask:
Bring a nice cup of tea to your wife,
For this will be every morning your task
Through all of our new married life."

"In married life," he replied, "both must share.
That's what I teach couples to learn.
If I make tea today dear, 'tis but fair
That tomorrow tea-making's your turn."

"As a priest," she said, "you should know, my dear
What the good Bible says if you look.
Tea-making's for men: this message is clear.
For He brews is the name of a book."

As marriages, even clerical ones, develop, differences and problems
may arise. This is shown in the next poem. This has been performed
with vicar and wife reading alternate verses. The wife leaves after the
first verse and returns holding a greenish-brown shopping bag.

11

Temptation

The vicar did not get much pay:
Balance at bank - alas! - was down.
He told his wife to keep away
From the smartest shop in town.

One day from shopping home she came
With plastic bag of greenish brown:
In golden letters was the name
Of the smartest shop in town.

The priest looked up: his work he stopped:
He gazed at her with worried frown:
"I hope," he said, "you have not shopped
At the smartest shop in town."

His wife with downcast eyes replied:
"I saw displayed a lovely gown.
Only to look I went inside
Of the smartest shop in town."

He said, "We cannot make ends meet:
Expenses are up and income down.
Avert your gaze, turn back your feet
From the smartest shop in town."

"I'm sad," he said, "That I should nag
About your coveting a gown.
Do you mean it's in that bag
From the smartest shop in town?"

She said, "Oh husband I confess -
I've put a large deposit down.
Your credit card has bought this dress
From the smartest shop in town."

"These wordly cares you must resist
If you would win the martyr's crown.
On simple clothes you should insist -
NOT from the smartest shop in town."

"It was just me - my shape - my size -
My colour too were in that gown.
I tried it on - 'twas such a prize
In the smartest shop in town."

"Temptation came and you gave way.
You ought to beat the Tempter down.
'Get behind me Satan' say
Tho' 'twas the smartest shop in town."

"I did! I firmly spoke my mind.
Said, 'Get behind the tempting gown.'
Satan obeyed and stood behind
In the smartest shop in town."

"If you spoke firmly as you ought
And Satan fled behind that gown,
Why do you hold a dress you've bought
From the smartest shop in town?"

"Because SHE said, 'Madame looks nice
Seen from behind in that smart gown.'
I took that salesgirl's good advice
In the smartest shop in town."

In our theme of Men and Women we now come to two tragic poems about the married life.

A Slight Mistake
A tragic ballad

A slight mistake in an email note
Cost poor Robert his life.
When to his friend and neighbour he wrote
"I'm sorry I borrowed your wife."

"It was only just for one single night
While you had gone away.
I thought for once it would be alright
And your wife said 'twas okay."

"Then I had lots of things on my brain
And time was getting late.
If you ask your wife she will explain
Just why I could not wait."

"Since no other person had what I seek
And my need was very great,
And mine would not be back for a week,
I simply could not wait."

"There is no damage or scratch you'll see
For I behaved with care.
No harm is done: I think you'll agree
That friends are meant to share."

His neighbour with grief and anger hot
Rushed to the house next door.
In jealous rage poor Robert he shot.
Left him dead upon the floor.

Envoi
He went back home with sorrow smitten
And found beside the door
Another note by Robert written,
Which he'd not seen before.

This note said, "Work had to be done.
Sorry about my gaffe.
I expect my email gave you both some fun
And a really good old laugh."

"What a funny mistake in the email I sent
When I wrote about things shared.
Of course wifi not wife I meant.
Mine was being repaired."

The Motor Car
A tragic ode

She drove from the back with a voice of scorn.
His car was rusting away.
The police flagged him down one summer morn
On a busy motorway.

"Sorry sir," they said, "to cause you grief.
Your wife fell out miles from here."
"Thank heaven that's all," he replied with relief.
"I'd gone quite deaf was my fear."

And now an extended version of The Motor Car in French…

La Voiture

Ballade de la vie conjugale

Très ancienne est la voiture
Qu'il conduit comme un fou.
Mais il ne sait pas (bien sûr) -
Le châssis a un trou.

Elle, toujours assise derrière,
La conduit comme une reine.
Commandant qu'il accélère,
Ou qu'il appliqué le frein.

Un jour le ciel était clair:
Ils sortirent en voiture.
Elle disait ce qu'il devait faire:
Lui - levres pincées, traits durs.

De parler elle ne cessa pas -
"Vas lentement!" "Vas vite!"
"Attention aux flâneurs là!"
"Soigneux - ou je te quitte!"

"Écoute mes mots, tu mallheureux!"
"Oh, tu n'entends je crois!"
"Regarde le changement des feux!"
"Gauche ici…. non… c'est droit."

"Change ici - première vitesse -
Une dangereuse descente."
"Mais change encore, ou tu cesses -
Faut pas conduire trop lent."

"Ici la rue est ascendante -
Comme sait tout le monde!
Longue, forte, et sineuse cette pente -
Vitesse…je crois, seconde."

"Òu est la carte? L'as-tu lue?
Oh! C'est une ville étrange!
J'ai grand faim. Nous sommes perdus!
Où le gateau que je mange?"

Soudain…silence…tout était calme:
C'était une paix profonde…
Ni mots, ni voix troublaient son âme…
Pas de paroles qui grondent.

C'était étrange: il sentit peur…
L'absence de cette voix…?
Il continua une demie-heure,
Mais en pensant: "Pourquoi?"

Décida - "Mais oui, j'accélère:
Retournons vite chez nous."
La Police, l'auto derrière,
Commande - "ARRETEZ-VOUS!"

"Monsieur, je vous informe -
C'est mon triste devoir -
Je sais - c'est tragédie enorme
Pour vous - if faut savoir."

"Ce châssis a un trou sans doute,
Puisque de cette voiture
Une dame est tombée sur la route.
Condoléances, Monsieur."

Il répondit: "Merci, mille fois!
Merci, Monsieur Gendarme!
Inespéré, vous donnez joie,
Et séchez toutes mes larmes."

"Tombée? Ma femme? La route? C'est rien!
C'est pas de coup affreux!
Une tragédie? Mais non! Tout bien!
Pour moi, c'est plus de peur."

"Monsieur, vous ôtez de mon coeur
Un fardeau grand et lourd.
Je pensais pour cette demi-heure -
JE SUIS DEVENU SOURD."

Deception

An ode...

The man in this verse was sixty-one,
A very rich man was he.
The girl her twenty-first year had begun,
A beautiful girl was she.

This beautiful girl became the man's bride
But on the day they were wed,
The best man called the bridegroom aside.
These were the words that he said -

"How did a fellow at your stage of life
- Sixty-one - wed such a belle?
Tell me your secret; I'ld love such a wife.
I'm an old friend - you can tell."

The bridegroom whispered, "She's lovely but dumb
And thinks I am much older.
For she's convinced I'm ninety-one
As that is what I told her."

"The answer you seek is now quite clear.
This poor girl hopes that she
In a very short time, maybe one year,
A merry rich widow will be."

...and a limerick

Alice was a lady lovely and fair.
All admired her elegant natural-look hair.
When asked how long she took
To get this beautiful look
Said, "My hairdresser does it when I am not there."

A Traditional Very Young Couple Revised

Misunderstandings: A shock for Jill's mother

A sweet little girl was dear Jill:
She said, "Oh mummy, Jack's mad.
He said when we walked up the hill
That I'm no girl but a lad."

"So how did you," mum asked, "answer back?"
This was the sweet girl's reply -
"To prove I'm a girl to friend Jack
I simply showed him my ...."

Sudden fear struck at Jill's mother
Who feared, upset and alarmed,
By what they'd shown to each other.
Jill might for ever be harmed.

Jill spoke on, but not knowing why
Mummy's face had then seemed to flip,
"...proved I'm a girl by showing him my
Card of Brownie membership."

Misunderstandings: A shock for Jack's mother

"We had secs today," said little Jack.
"Me and Jill thought 'twas fun."
When mum heard this her face looked black.
She thought, "What have they done?"

In her mind a letter to the press
And one to Jack's school head.
Heedless of mother's deep distress,
Continuing, Jack said -

"Though some boring stuff we had to learn,
At lunch (he licked his lips)
SECOND HELPING was our class's turn,
And it was fish and chips."

A Traditional Very Old Couple Revised

Darby and Joan
An ode

Puer furens
impressit memorem dente labris notan
Horace. Odes 1:13
The frenzied boy impressed the mark on (your) lips with his teeth.

To her Darby said Joan in their ninetieth year,
Curled up together in bed for the night,
"Would you do as you did in our young days my dear?
Give me once again on my lips a nice bite?"

"Oh my darling, don't go, please don't leave me alone,"
She cried in alarm as he crept from her side.
"I'm off to the bathroom, don't you worry my Joan,
Just to fetch my false teeth," the old fellow replied.

Darby and Joan
A ballad
A man should be about twenty years older than his wife.
Aristotle: Politics 7:16

Now Darby planned to celebrate
For seventy-five was he.
His dear wife Joan, his lifelong mate
Just this same age was she.

His godmother, a fairy came
And said, "I promise you
Whatever birthday wish you name,
I'll make that wish come true."

Now Darby saw his dear wife Joan
And thought ('tis sad but truth)
"No more has she, what once she'd shown
The blush of early youth."

He saw some wrinkles on her face,
He saw ('tis hard to say)
Of sparkle in her eyes no trace.
Hair thin and grown quite grey.

In Aristotle once he'd read
For th'ideal married life
A man should have (that wise man said)
A twenty years' younger wife.

Oh reader, shed thy plenteous tears
At Darby's treacherous crime.
He said, "I want a wife whose years
Are twenty less than mine."

The fairy said, "I'll keep my word,
For fairy's word's a bond.
Because your birthday wish I heard
I'll wave my magic wand."

Her magic wand the fairy waved.
Old Darby felt inspired.
Although she felt he was depraved
She did what he desired.

Envoi
Thus Darby's birthday wish achieved
The perfect married life,
As he desired, he now received
A twenty years' younger wife.

For Joan, his wife, remained the same,
Seventy five was she,
Twenty years older he became,
Aged ninety-five was he.

Rustic Joe's Looking Glass
A nonsensical ballad

Rustic Joe Brown was very old
And wrinkled was his face.
Few teeth he had; if truth be told,
His beard was a disgrace.

His wife was just as old as he
And only had one tooth.
Wrinkled her face and one could see
She'd lost the bloom of youth.

In fields remote they lived alone.
Simple their life indeed.
They'd never seen and did not own
The things that most folk need.

A looking glass this lonely pair
Did never see or own
And so their own reflections there
Were quite a sight unknown.

It happened that this old Joe Brown
Some business had one day.
He rode into the nearest town
Full thirty miles away.

His business done, his time was free.
A tour of shops he made.
For sale in one, what did he see?
A looking glass displayed!

22

He felt then as he stopped and gazed,
"Oh what a great surprise!"
Standing quite still, he stood amazed.
Could scarce believe his eyes!

He saw the wrinkled face, the beard,
And thought (though this seems mad)
"To find this here is very weird -
A painting - my old dad!"

He thought, "Good business here I've done,
So I have cash to spare.
I'll spend a bit of what I've won
To buy that painting there."

He went inside; the glass he bought.
It made him very glad
To have what he - remember! - thought
Was painting of his dad.

He said, "My wife, she need not know.
She loved not dad, though dead.
I won't this painting to her show
But hang it in my shed."

He hung the glass up in his shed:
He'd played there as a lad.
Each day he went to look and said,
"Good morning," to his dad.

His wife now wondered why he went
Each day to that same place.
She sniffed his coat for smell of scent
Or some strange woman's trace.

She thought, "A secret Joe won't share.
Must be what I suspect.
He's got some fancy woman there
Whom I will soon detect."

So when her Joe had gone away
To work upon his land,
To his old shed she made her way,
Opened with trembling hand.

She opened the shed, of course to find
The glass: was horrified.
Nasty suspicions in her mind
Were fully justified.

There she stood and gazed, not daring
To move, so deep her rage.
A woman's face she saw now staring,
And wrinkled with old age.

Envoi
At last she turned away and cried,
Anger and grief combined,
"He's got some woman on the side.
Her picture here I find!"

"Perhaps he meets her in this place.
But what an awful sight!
Balding, one tooth, and wrinkled face.
Old, ugly, what a sight!"

"The reason why he's so obsessed
I simply cannot see.
When always has my Joe possessed
A lovely girl like me!"

The Handyman and the Spinster
A ballad concerning an insult and the dreadful revenge that followed
Old Alf had a handcart with his name
For a handyman was he.
Old Nell was a nosey spinster dame,
A dreadful gossip was she.

Old Nell accosted old Alf one day
And these words she spoke to him.
"I saw your handcart last Saturday
Parked outside the village inn."

"'Twas there three hours and a half outside
That Inn, 'White Hen and the Cock.'
Now this timing cannot be denied
For I checked it by my clock."

"Oh! Think of the precious hours you waste,
Of the hard-earned cash you spend.
A dissipated, drunken disgrace!
Your wicked ways you must mend."

By these words aroused , Alf replied, irate,
"From nosey ways you must turn.
I'm no disgrace, I tell you straight,
Though it's none of your concern."

"My handcart by the inn was standing.
I was working, bills to pay.
For I a new laid floor was sanding
Which took me half the day."

To get a just revenge Alf waited,
Thought, puffing at his fag,
"Old Nell will look so dissipated
.Other gossips' tongues will wag."

Envoi. Old Alf moved his handcart with his name.
Parked it soon as darkness fell.
Left it all night 'til the morning came
Right outside the house of Nell.

and finally…
A Love that dare now speak its name
A ballad

We lads were drinking the Bullingdon wine.
Our hearts were merry and gay.
I said to my lover, "Life would be fine
If we could marry one day."

Beneath the shade of the old dreaming spires
We dreamt in our youthful way,
But sadly we thought, in spite of love's fires,
We never would marry one day.

Then up spoke friend Dave, a slur in his voice,
(By wine he was carried away),
"I promise, dear friends, one day you'll rejoice.
You will be married one day."

"Sure as I'm drinking this Bullingdon wine
I promise to find you a way.
Then you, my dear friends, at last will be free
To marry each other one day."

"I'm a forceful man whom no one will stop,
Even those old men in grey.
In a modernised Party I'll rise to the top.
Then you will marry one day."

"All Natural Law and all Law Divine,
I'll throw the whole lot away.
I swear by the life of this Bullingdon wine
You'll marry each other one day."

We staggered back to our College for sleep
At the close of that fateful day.
For we knew that friend Dave his promise would keep
And we would marry one day.

We never lost hope as the long years passed,
Our hearts still merry and gay.
For we knew that the time would come at last
When we would marry one day.

Then friend Dave rose to the top at last
And fought for us in the fray.
The Bill which by Commons and Lords was passed
Allows us to marry this day.

We knew that friend Dave his promise had kept
Made on that fateful day.
Tears of relief and of joy we now wept
As we fixed our wedding day.

Envoi
How thankful we are for that Bullingdon wine
When hearts were merry and gay.
For we lads when all has turned out so fine
Were married last Saturday.

The Natural and Unnatural World is the theme from pages 28 to 69.

The first three look at life from the viewpoint of birds and animals.
Following the verses on Men and Women, the first looks at the attitude
of birds to people.

At the Aviary
An ode

Thoughts of the visitors
We stand very still to get a brief sight
Of exotic birds on the wing.
We stop and listen with silent delight
To the merry songs which they sing.

But then we thought as we read each long name
On the plaques and the fence that confined them,
"To keep these birds enclosed, it seems such a shame.
Nature for wild life designed them."

Thoughts of the birds
We aviary birds fly from tree top to tree,
Flash feathers with coloured glow.
We sing out for joy; we're fed, safe and free,
But who are these creatures below?

We thought of those folk who just stand and stare
Through the wire fence that confines them.
To keep humans enclosed seems sad and unfair.
Nature for freedom designed them.

The Dog and TV
An ode

I sat with my folk on Saturday night
While watching a play on TV
Where one of the cast to my great delight
Was a lovely big dog (like me!)

He was walking along from left to right
For a really live dog was he.
At the edge of the set he vanished from sight.
I wondered, "Where can that dog be?"

I stood up and sniffed our big TV screen,
Then thoughtfully walked round behind,
But no trace of that dog was smelt or was seen,
No trace of that dog did I find.

I'd seen him, I'm sure - or was it a dream
Or trick played by strange humankind?
Things in this world are not quite what they seem.
It's all very odd to my mind.

The Pigeons
A sonnet

As I put out food for the birds every morning I wondered how they feel when I am away.

Us pigeons come for our breakfast at eight
When some magic brings what all pigeons need.
On tree branch or roof top singing we wait
For three little piles of our wild bird seed.
Us pigeons nod up and down with small heads,
The jackdaws come to eat and to chatter.
Clever magpies duck in water stale breads
Small birds, a thrush and robin, eat later.
But sometimes for several days in a row
No food appears, we screech loudly in vain
Why this should happen, us pigeons don't know.
After some days it appears once again.
Because my brain, like my head is quite small,
I simply can't understand it at all.

The next part of our Natural and Unnatural World is concerned with horticulture.

We begin with an ode.

The Old Gardener

The gardener had grown very old
And very, very slow.
Slowly he did as he was told.
Would slowly come and go.

One day, with very heavy tread,
He stamped upon the earth.
He squashed a snail until 'twas dead,
Chuckling with silent mirth.

Some people said, "You had no need
To squash that snail to bits.
It was a very savage deed.
A snail to sin commits."

He said, "That snail was driving me
Out of my poor old mind.
For where I walk I always see
Him following close behind."

The Young Gardener or alternatively
Pest Control

The gardener was a simple boy.
A simple boy was he.
One day his master said, "Now Roy,
Just do this job for me."

"You see these little heaps of soil?
They're not a pretty sight.
Made by a mole who came to spoil
My lawn at dead of night."

"I want you now to do your best
By any means you know
To rid me of this little pest.
Good lad, now off you go."

A week went past, Roy said, "For sure
Your honour will be glad.
You need not worry any more.
I'm not a simple lad."

"Oh no, I am a cunning chap.
I gave that mole a fright!
I bought a very special trap
And caught the pest one night."

"And then I dug a neat round hole
And so he won't survive
Took out that little pesky mole
And buried him alive!"

I translated **The Young Gardener** into German as best I could, trying to keep the same metre and rhyming scheme.

Der Gartner war ein dummer Knab',
Oh ja, er war sehr dumm.
Der Meister sagte, "Hans, ich hab'
Für dich, Arbeit zu tun."

"Du siehst die kleinen Haufen hier,
Vom Maulwurfen gemacht:
Den Garten ruinert der Tier,
Der kommt hier jede Nacht."

"Tue was du kannst, befehle ich:
Entferne diesen Weh!
Die Weise macht nicht aus für mich,
Mein Knabe Hans, nun geh!"

Nach Tagen drei am früh'n Morgen
Kam Knabe Hans züruck.
"Ganz vorbei, mein Herr, die Sorgen:
Ich bringe Freud' und Gluck!"

Bin nicht dumm; klüger als alle,
Sehr schlau hab'ich gekauft
Eine Sondermauklwurffalle:
Er hat darin gelauft.

"Ich grabte (für die Strafe fest)
Ein Loch sehr tief und rund,
Beerdigte die böse Pest
Lebendige im grund!"

Our German conversation group put the German version onto a machine for translation back into English. This was the result:

The gardener was an easier young.
He was a simple boy.
One day his master "Roy," said now
"Make only this job for me."

"You see this little pile of soil."
You are not a pretty sight -
Made by a mole, who came to spoil
"My lawn in the dead of night."

"I would like to now do your best you"
You know how
To get rid these little plague me:
"Good lad - now go."

A week passed, Roy said, "sure"
Her honour will be glad.
You need no longer worry -
"I am not a simple boy."

"Oh no, I am a cunning CHAP."
I gave a fright this mole!
I bought a special trap
"Everyone caught the plague one night."

"And then I dug a clean round hole."
And so he does not überleben -
Took this pesky MAULWURF
"AND HIM ALIVE BURIED!"

The Obsessive Gardener
A ballad

Old George had been, both man and lad,
A gardener enthusiastic.
He was so keen, folk thought him mad.
Some called him a fanatic.

To sow and plant and till the ground
Supplied the love he needed.
This gardening passion, old George found,
All other loves exceeded.

To a gardening mate he came to lend
A hand to assist one day.
So George was working with his friend.
A lawn of turf to lay.

Then suddenly a hearse passed by
To the crematorium.
George stood still, capless, with a sigh,
For a moment silent, dumb.

"I am surprised," said George's mate,
"At the respect you show.
Was the departed someone great
Or a friend from long ago?"

Envoi
"My respect," George said, "which you have seen,
I believe was right, for she
For over fifty years had been
A perfect wife to me."

The Lament of the Garden Gnomes
A sonnet

We garden gnomes know of the Chelsea Show:
The catalogue we saw and magazine.
Not only were there natural plants that grow,
But manmade artefacts were strangely seen.
A boat race garden having shields and oars,
Large coloured spheres attract the puzzled eye:
Statues of rabbits, birds and big wild boars,
Things made of bronze or stone for all to buy.
But only we, the little folk, are banned,
Though with our smiling face and hat to cheer,
Beside a pool with fishing rod we stand,
Or through the sunlit summer flowers we peer.
So we, the garden gnomes, would like to know,
Why we are banned from every Chelsea Show.

This sonnet was written in 2004 when garden gnomes were not allowed
in gardens at the Chelsea Flower Show.

Down on the Farm
Three pages of lyrics, odes and limericks.

Hail to Thee, Blithe Sparrer!

A Cockney girl a lark did espy,
Its sweet melodious sound
As it hovered in the summer sky
Filled all the world around.

"That sparrer's stuck!" called the girl from town.
"Please come 'ere, Miss, you must.
It can't get up and it can't get down.
It's 'ollering fit to bust."

The Cockerel

The cockerel was chasing the hen with mad lust:
By her beauty he was taken.
He suddenly stopped to eat crumbs and a crust
When the table cloth was shaken.

The old farmer saw this and in astonishment said,
"As a lad (believe you my word),
I'd never have stopped for a few crumbs of bread
If I were chasing some bird."

Secret Love

Let's escape to the fields and the farms, lover dear,
But speak softly and come in disguise,
For each stalk of corn has more than one ear
And potatoes have very keen eyes.

Old Rustic Joe Again from page 22

Old Joe hit his horse with a stick
Which made the poor horse very sick
Down he fell, quite dead.
In surprise Joe said,
"'Tis first time he's played such a trick."

The Romantic Bees

Oh! How romantic are some men,
Full worthy of an ode.
Their love they consummate and then
The earth seems to explode.

Some bees are more romantic mates,
Worthy of better odes.
For when his love he consummates
This bee himself explodes.

Mary and the Bull

Along a country lane in Devon
Young Mary led a bull one day.
Although the lass was only seven,
Yet she could make the bull obey.

"She seems too small," thought a passer-by.
He asked, "Where d'you take that bull my dear?"
"To serve our cows," came the girl's reply,
"In our field not far from here."

"But 'tis work that needs a grown man, strong.
Why not your father, may I ask?"
With a solemn face she said, "That's wrong.
The bull, not dad, must do this task."

The Seed Potato
A foretaste of "The Unnatural World" section.

A young seed potato was feeling life flat,
So he said to his friends round him on the mat,
"While here we all sit
In order to chit
Let's cheer up our lives with a bit of chit chat."

Henry and his Fish
A ballad

Now Henry was a lonely lad.
A goldfish he possessed.
The friends he knew all thought him mad.
He loved his goldfish best.

To watch his fish was his delight.
It swam so calm and free.
He thought, entrancèd by this sight,
None better would he see.

For love he had no other need.
He took no girl to dine.
Content was he his fish to feed
(And save the price of wine).

He called his fish, was sure it heard,
When summoned by its name.
Although it answered not a word,
It soothed poor Henry's brain.

Yet Henry had an awful fear
Which would not go away.
His fish was ill, it did appear.
He worried night and day..

So Henry took his bowl with fish
And went off to the vet.
"My fish is ill," he said, "I wish
Your good advice to get."

40

"I hope you'll put my mind at rest.
I'm right out of my wits.
I'm sure my fish has some disease
Like epileptic fits."

With expert eye the vet surveyed
The fish. "From what I see
You have no need to be afraid.
He looks quite well to me."

Envoi
"Oh yes, in water he's okay,"
Replied the tearful lad.
"I take him out to stroke and play
And then he goes quite mad."

In this section on "The Natural and Unnatural World" the theme on pages 42 - 57 is Hunting, Shooting and Fishing.

A Mythological Hunter from Ovid: Met. 3: 138 - 252

Forth went Actaeon, Hunter bold,
With fierce hounds a stag to slaughter.
By chance, or fate, he did behold
Diana by a pool of water.

The bathing costumes which we wear
Had not at that time been invented.
As Diana and her nymphs were bare,
On Actaeon her wrath she vented.

Because he'd got her to such shame
The goddess used her magic skill.
Poor Actaeon a stag became,
Whom his own hounds did hunt and kill.

Fair maids! Do not uncloth'd recline
By water's edge, nor naked swim,
Lest man who sees thy form divine
Leads thee to cast a spell on him.

Oh youths and men! Shouldst thou surprise
Some naked nymphs by pool or sea.
Turn back thy gaze, avert thy eyes,
Lest Actaeon's fate should fall on thee.

The Royal Hunters. *A short ode*

George the Fifth and his son, folk tell,
Did not get on very well.
But the king with his son and heir
Had one interest they could share.
Chasing the birds gave both delight
But with a different aim in sight.
George shot his birds with bits of lead
While Edward took his birds to bed.

The ballad on the next page continues the aristocratic note, but apart from verse 1 and the Countryman quotation has no reference to any actual earl.

The Hunting Earl. *A ballad*

Verse 1: Suggested by an older priest who told me in 1950 that in his undergraduate time, the Master of Magdelene announced, "Lord [I forget who] has failed his exams: on the other hand he is the Master of the Beagles."
Verse 7: A quotation in The Countryman of March 2017, "Hunting for spectacles is the only sport left in old age." (Lord Grey of Falloden 1862-1955).

The Hunting Earl. *A ballad*

The youthful earl who at studies was slack
In the Oxford college was Master
Of the very popular Beagle pack.
In hunting none other was faster.

On leaving Oxford his joy knew no bounds.
He thought he had travelled to heaven.
Invited by friends to stag hunts with hounds.
Some in Scotland, others in Devon.

To Europe he travelled with his first post
As part of the Diplomatic Corps.
On many days off he went with his host
In deep woods to hunt the wild boar.

On duty's call he next travelled out East
When the old Raj was still holding sway.
Hunting with princes he chased a new beast.
The fierce tiger was now his chief prey.

When his diplomatic life did expire
He returned to his own native land.
He hunted the fox across the broad shire
Twice a week until hunting was banned.

He travelled each day around his flower bed
Inspecting the leaves of each lily.
Hunting the beetle, small, shiny, bright red
(Though this tiger hunter felt silly!)

Envoi: Old age came at last as it comes to us all,
E'en for keen eyed hunters time passes.
He travels now through his ancestral hall,
And hunts for his lost pair of glasses!

George the Hunter. *A ballad*
Now George he was a hunting man
In the deep frozen North.
With water hot in Thermos can
And food, he once set forth.

He hoped a polar bear to kill
Whose fur would make a coat.
Whose flesh his wife with homely skill
Would cook for Sunday roast.

The suddenly a bear appeared,
White as the snow around.
Brave huntsman George was not afraid
But firmly stood his ground.

He took his stand as he'd been taught
In the correct position.
Then realised he had not brought
His pack of ammunition.

This was to George, resourceful man,
Nothing but a trifle.
He filled with water from his can
The barrel of his rifle.

He gave the trigger then a squeeze.
Through th'air the water spread.
The cold air made the water freeze
As hard as any lead.

Like bullet flying through the air
As to its target fated,
It went straight to the polar bear
Whose head it penetrated.

Envoi
Then once inside the bear's warm head
It melted back again.
The bear dropped down at once quite dead
Of water on the brain!

44

The next three poems are about fishing.
The second one has a longer version in French, as in the poem "La Voiture" on pages 16 and 17.
If the fishermen, one particularly, do not seem very bright, this is not due to any bias against fishermen. It was simply needed to make nonsensical verse.

Country Fishing.
A ballad

Fred and Bill set out one day.
The day was bright and fine.
By country lanes they made their way
With rod and bait and line.

Now a very clever lad was Fred
But Bill was not too bright.
"We'll find a river soon," they said,
"And things will be alright."

After three miles a bridge they met
Over a deep stream's flow.
Two men sat on the parapet
To catch the fish below.

"We can do that," remarked bright Fred.
"We'll even better go."
"I'll sit and hold your feet," he said
"And dangle you below."

For two more miles the couple trod,
Another bridge to meet.
As Bill held out his line and rod
Fred held him by the feet.

Said Fred, "Keep still, don't be afraid.
Shout quickly, 'Time to stop!'
When a good catch of fish you've made
I'll pull you to the top."

For two full hours Bill dangled 'til
He thought his arms would drop.
Then with a cry, sudden and shrill,
He called out, "TIME TO STOP!"

"You've caught a fish?" called happy Fred.
"Our plan has turned out right."
(Remember that it has been said -
Poor Bill was not too bright.")

"NO! NO!" screamed Bill, "PULL UP AGAIN!"
Shrieked Bill. "HELP! PULL ME BACK!
"HELP! HELP! HERE COMES A TRAIN
ALONG THIS RAILWAY TRACK."

Winter Fishing
A ballad

Now Bill had heard that Eskimos,
Who like a tasty dish,
Break ice - for oft their waters froze -
To catch a nice fat fish.

Winter was very hard one year.
"I'll try it now," thought Bill.
Pick-axe he took with fishing gear
And planned to eat his fill.

He soon came to a frozen lake,
Whose ice was thick and strong.
It took his weight: it did not break.
"This won't," thought Bill, "take long."

His axe he raised: it's heavy blow
That solid ice would smash:
He swung it round, then struck it down.
It made a mighty crash.

Some people skating on the lake
Were startled by the sound.
But Bill a little hole did make
- Quite neat and almost round.

He took his rod with steady hand,
Fixed with his chosen bait.
He lowered it, and took his stand,
and settled down to wait.

The suddenly a voice he heard.
It struck his heart with fear.
No man he saw but just a word,
"THERE ARE NO FISH IN HERE!"

It echoed in the air around.
Again it came, then thrice.
A disembodied warning sound -
"NO FISH BENEATH THIS ICE!"

Loudspeakers sounded overhead.
"YOU THERE - WHY DON'T YOU THINK?!
I AM THE MANAGER," it said,
"IN CHARGE OF THIS ICE RINK."

La Grande Aventure de Guillaume:
Amour et Tristesse d'un Pêcheur

Guillaume, homme simple et peu savant,
Evitait livres et lettres.
Un grand amour, fou et puissant,
Possédait tout son être.

Pour fille, pour femme, nulle passion
Inspirait ses désirs:
Dans son loisir une action
Donnait immense plaisir.

Son grand amour, c'était la pêche.
Elle remplait tout son coeur.
Journée humide ou journée seche
Ne lui donnait peur.

Avec amorce, pliant et ligne,
Son panier sous le bras,
Brave pécheur, de ce nom tout digne,
Il marchait à ferme pas.

La riviére, le lac, le fleuve,
Eau clair ou pleine de boue,
Soleil ou brume ou nuages qui pleuvent -
Guillaume les aimait tous.

Saumon, morue, carpe ou truite…
Bien connus ou nouveaux…
Poissons du lac, de mer les fruits…
Guillaume les pensait beaux.

Enfin une tragédie! Helas!
Un très, très dur hiver.
Partout le neige, eau gelée, glace,
Partout le froid sevère.

Guillaume éprouva telle tristesse,
Sa figure morne à voir,
Qu'un ami, voyant sa détresse,
L'incita à l'espoir.

"Guillaume, ami, rappelez-vous:
Que font les Esquimaux?"
"Dans la glace ils frappent un trou
Pour y pêcher dans l'eau."

Guillaume, suivant ce bon avis,
Un grand marteau trouva:
Avec amorce et ligne sortit,
Son panier sous le bras,

Trouva un lac. "Voici la place!"
Eau gelée, ferme et dure,
Marcha droit au centre de cette glace,
Commença l'aventure.

Il frappa, frappa, de toute force,
Et fit un beau rond trou,
Jeta la ligne avec amorce
Dans l'abîme noir dessous.

Il attendait avec espérance.
D'abord tout semblait bien.
Espérait avoir de la chance,
Mais il attrapa - rien!

Puis soudain a-t-il entendu
Une voix, ni douce, ni belle,
Étrange, dans l'air, là, suspendue,
Une voix surnaturelle.

La voix qui parla en rudes mots
Rompit ce Paradis.
"Hé! Pas de poissons dans cette eau!"
Mystérieuse, elle dit.

Autour il vit des patineurs
De lui insouciants,
Encore il pêchait - moins heureux -
Mais encore espérant.

Puis retentissante dans l'espace
Pour la deuxième fois -
"Hé! Pas de poissons sous cette glace!"
- Cette haute, mystérieuse voix.

Agité, triste en son esprit,
Mais suivant l'aventure,
Guillaume pensait des mots qu'a dit
Cette voix affreuse et dure.

"Hé! Pas de poissons sous cette glace!"
Encore! La troisième fois!
Les mots résonnaient par l'espace -
Nul parlant peut - il voir.

"Monsieur! Vous! Hé! Soyez plus sage!"
Ces mots inspirent la peur.
"Vous n' êtes pas ici a la plage!
Ecoutez! Toute à l'heure -

Mes yeux cherchent tout, de long en large.
Je vois chaque homme… et vous!
Cette glace est faite pour patinage
Qu'a gâté votre trou.

Ice vous etes au patinoir,
Et moi le directeur."
Une microphone diffuse cette voix
Qui lui donnait peur.

FIN
du
Poème

Sea Fishing

At the start of sunny weather
Bill and Joe and Fred all three
Set off for a week together,
Booked some rooms beside the sea.

As they strolled, anticipating
What the day might hold in store,
Saw a board with notice stating,
"Boats for hire" beside the shore.

They said, on looking at this board,
"Here's a change from stream and lake.
The price is one we can afford.
Let's decide which boat to take."

Bill and Fred each took an oar,
Rowing hard with strength and skill,
They quickly reached some miles from shore,
For the sea was calm and still.

Well out at sea Fred looked around.
"Here's a likely spot," he said.
It was a place where fish abound -
(A skilful angler was old Fred).

They settled down with rod and line,
Each resolved to show his skill.
Each caught some fish, full, fat and fine.
"Whoppers," called out Fred to Bill.

"Good lads," "Well done," "What a catch!"
Chuckled all with happy glee.
"One we'll put in Angling Match
And the others eat for tea."

To celebrate each drank six beers.
(Eighteen cans were in a pack.)
Shouting grew loud: "Good lads" and "Cheers!"
And, "Tomorrow we'll come back."

So they planned to come tomorrow
To this special place they'd found.
Planned again a boat to borrow,
For the place where fish abound.

Fred pondered with a look of pain.
Then said, "There's one snag I've thought.
How shall we find this spot again
Where these lovely fish we've caught?"

Six cans of beer excited Joe.
Leaning o'er board, big ticks he wrote.
"These ticks." he said, "this spot will show
On th'outside of the fishing boat."

Happy they rowed back to shore.
Happy they ate fish for tea.
Happy they planned to catch some more.
Happy dreams came to all three.

Envoi
Next day a fishing boat they hired
From the man down on the quay.
Keenly they rowed with hearts inspired
Out across the sunlit sea.

Then suddenly Bill screamed, "Oh shame!
We'll not find that special spot.
This boat's not ticked! It's not the same!
It's a different boat we've got!"

Pages 54 to 69 contain the Unnatural World part of this section. There are verses about talking animals and birds.

In the first poem Frank has a less happy ending than George in the previous one on page 44. It contains serious advice - be careful what you pray for.

Frank and the Talking Bear
A tragic ballad

Now Frankie was a hunting man
Who loved a hunting life.
So he would set out on his own
With rifle and with knife.

No deep belief our Frank possessed.
His faith was very small.
The truth must surely be confessed.
He had no faith at all.

But he had friends whose faith profound
Encouraged them to say,
Since dangers did his life surround,
Frank ought to learn to pray.

Heedless of them, Frank left one day,
Saying he had nothing feared.
Then suddenly, blocking his way,
A great big bear appeared.

Grizzly this bear, a fearful sight,
Looking for food to eat.
Frank knew that if he took to flight
The bear had faster feet.

Frank raised his rifle for a kill.
Alas! What rotten luck!
In spite of all his huntsman's skill,
The wretched rifle stuck.

With deep foreboding sense of dread
Then in his deep despair,
Frank thought of words his friends had said
And uttered his first prayer -

That this bear might that faith believe
Which friends had tried to share,
His fierce and savage ways to leave
And be a pious bear.

Envoi
O wondrous thing! Frank's prayer was heard.
With paws together placing,
The bear knelt down and spoke this word,
His eyes upward facing -

"Now I'm a bear who does believe
In gratitude I thank thee
For this food I will receive,"
And then he ate poor Frankie.

The Talking Cow
A ballad

George drove along a country road
By fields which cows did crop.
When suddenly his motor slowed
And shuddered to a stop.

George stepped outside and then undid
A catch with skilful hand.
With care he raised the bonnet lid,
The fault to understand.

He poked around and looked to see,
Then to his wife he said,
"The fault - it must the battery be.
I think it looks quite dead."

"That's not as bad as it might be.
I bought it this last spring.
The battery's under guarantee,
And won't cost me a thing."

What happened next was very weird.
George had a great surprise.
Over the nearby hedge appeared
A head with poking eyes.

The head was of a speckled cow
Who said, "I saw you halt.
I've studied cars and tell you now -
It's not the battery's fault."

The speaking cow gave George a shock.
She mooed, then spoke again.
"I heard the engine give a knock.
The battery's not to blame."

"Because you have a worn-out clutch,
It won't go into gear.
So I can say for sure this much -
Repairs will be quite dear."

George hurried to the old Farm House
And found the farmer there.
Then with the farmer and his spouse
His strange news he did share.

"I scarce believed what I did hear.
You cow spoke! - said my clutch
Had gone. I must replace my gear,
For which repairs cost much."

The farmer listened, plucked his brow,
Thinking of what he heard.
Then asked, "Was it a speckled cow
Who spoke this troubling word?"

"Yes, yes," said George, "Black, speckled, white."
The farmer said, "I guessed!
That's my cow Buttercup all right,
But set your mind at rest."

Envoi
"You have no cause to worry now,
For - clever though she seems,
And talks a lot, - she's not the cow
Who knows about machines."

The Helpful Bees
A ballad

Bill's car once on a country lane
Came to a sudden halt.
A queen bee on the window pane
Said, "Tell me what's the fault?"

Surprised, Bill said in great dismay,
"A sad, sad situation -
We're out of petrol miles away
From any petrol station."

Queen bee replied with friendly buzz
"I'll bring some help old chap.
Just do one thing - no need to fuss -
Undo the petrol cap."

She flew away, flew back and brought
More bees upon the wing.
Bill's wife was scared because she thought
The bees were going to sting.

Not so! Down through the petrol spout,
Whose cap Bill did unscrew,
Into the petrol tank and out
Each bee in turn then flew.

When all the rest away had flown
Into their hive to rest,
The queen bee, who remained alone,
To Bill these words addressed,

"Now try again the starter switch.
My bees gave what you need."
Doubtful, Bill tried the starter, which
Did straightaway succeed.

Bill said, "You and your bees we thank,
Though this seems so funny.
What did they do? I know my tank
Does not run on honey."

Envoi
Queen said, "I know a petrol's name,
So each one did a wee.
I thought the produce was the same,
And supplied you with Bee Pee."

The Ballad of Tim, the Talking Dog

Old Albert had a dog called Tim,
Of whom he was so proud.
He took him to a local inn,
Where dogs were not allowed.

He went up to the bar and tried
A whisky there to buy.
"The notice said, 'NO DOGS INSIDE,'"
Came the innkeeper's reply.

"But this dog is a special kind.
He can talk when needed.
He has a human voice and mind,
So let him stay," Bill pleaded.

The innkeeper said, "If you can show
That what you claim is right,
Your dog can stay and you won't owe
For what you drink tonight."

Bert said, "I'll give the proof you need.
Three questions I will pose.
Then Tim, who is a special breed,
Will answer all he knows."

"First question then," old Albert said.
"So we can stay inside.
What is that thing above my head?"
"ROOF - WOOF," the dog replied.

"One right!" said Bert, "Now tell us, Tim,
Your answer if you know.
With what do we play the violin?"
The dog replied, "BOW - WOW."

"Give me a great composer's name,
Who famous music wrote."
Without a pause the answer came,
"BACH - BARK," from Tim's deep throat.

"He answered first, then second, third,"
Claimed Albert with a grin.
"Now since he spoke the proper word,
We need not leave your inn."

The innkeeper said, "Your test's a spoof
For BACH and ROOF and BOW.
Are normal doggie sounds not proof.
So outside you must go."

Envoi
So Bert and Tim must leave the inn:
It was a cruel fate.
But then the last words came from Tim.
Alas! They were too late.

Tim said, "I'm very sorry I
Stopped you having whisky.
Instead of Bach my last reply
Should have been 'Stravinski.'"

Two Dogs and a Cat: *A lyrical poem*

Two dogs and a cat set out one day
To a famous concert hall.
With instruments they hoped to play
In the coming festival.

"We've come," they said, "upon a mission
To your famous concert hall.
So please may we have an audition
For the coming festival."

The conductor said, a smile on his face,
In that famous concert hall,
"But dogs and cats can have no place
In our coming festival."

One dog replied, "Listen, please hark
In your famous concert hall.
I'm a dog who'll play a loud Bach
In your coming festival."

Then the second dog put in his word
In that famous concert hall.
"I Offenbach and so would be heard
In your coming festival."

The cat next made a special claim
In that famous concert hall.
"I'm de pussy, a well-known name
For your coming festival."

The answer came, "Each made good reason
In my famous concert hall,
So I'll book you for the whole new season
In the coming festival."

"I'll advertise, 'A SPECIAL EVENT
In this famous CONCERT HALL'
And charge an extra supplement
In the coming festival."

The Two Hens

The Lady Mayoress had once laid a stone
In the wall of the Civic Centre,
On which the opening event was shown
To inform all folk as they enter.

Although this stone was a hard, heavy weight,
A man's skilful hand had engraved it.
There clearly was shown the name, with the date,
Of the Mayoress who had laid it.

Two hens who'd escaped from the Free Range Farm,
Where to lay large eggs was their duty,
Wandered in, studied these words with alarm,
In spite of their grace, charm and beauty.

One hen exclaimed, "Oh poor Mayoress!
Just think what that stone must be weighing!
Imaging the pain, oh think of the stress
When that great, big stone she was laying!"

Auntie Meg's Parrot
An ode

A parrot belonged to old Auntie Meg.
He was her pride and delight.
When one said, "Hullo," he raised his left leg.
And at, "Good-bye," raised his right.

"What if one says, 'Hello,'" asked a bright young wit,
"As another says, 'Goodbye?'"
"I fall off me perch you silly young twit,"
Was the parrot's prompt reply.

A ballad

Aunt Meg her parrot loved so well,
He was her precious bird.
But yet sometimes, the truth to tell,
He used a naughty word.

One day he like a trooper swore
Which made poor Meg upset.
She said, "If you say that one time more
Some punishment you'll get."

"Inside the fridge, so dark and cold,
Three hours you'll have to spend.
Don't say that you have not been told.
That's where bad birds we send."

The parrot all the following week
Lived in so great a fear
That no bad words came from his beak,
Just, "Bother" and, "Oh dear."

Then suddenly he felt so mad
He shrieked for all to hear
A string of words so foul and bad
We cannot print them here.

Aunt Meg was faithful to her word
Although it caused her pain.
Into the fridge she put her bird.
Three hours he must remain.

Now Christmas was not far away
When people celebrate.
So in Meg's fridge a turkey lay
All trussed up on a plate.

Three long hours the parrot passed
In prison cold and grim,
Until Aunt Meg returned at last,
Opened the fridge for him.

He came out changed, we must confess.
All shiv'ring from the cold,
His feathers in a tangled mess,
The beak not quite so bold.

Envoi
After a while, although still weak,
He raised a mournful head.
In falt'ring tones began to speak,
And this is what he said -

"As punishment because I curse,
Three hours in jail I served.
What awful sin is so much worse
Which more severe deserved?

"For I found another bird in there
Who could not move one bit:
His feathers gone, he was quite bare.
What sin did he commit?"

Here is a French version of the previous poem.

Le Perroquet qui Parle

Madame avait un grand oiseau
Qu'elle aimait comme une mère -
Un perroquet très vif, très beau -
Elle était très fière.

Elle l'appelait, "Mon cher Trésor":
Ses yeux brillaient comme feu,
Ses plumes luisaient colorées d'or,
D'orange, de rouge, de bleu.

Cet oiseau souvent imitait
Ce qu'il entendait dire:
Madame ses amies invitait
Pour parler, puis pour rire.

Un jour il avait entendu
Des gros mots, pas très purs!
Il imita - "C'est défendu,"
Dit-elle: "Mon cher, tu jures."

"Si vilains mots, si méchant son,
Tu dis encore une fois,
Dans "Le Frigo" pour ta prison
Passer trois heures tu dois!"

Cet oiseau voulait rester libre,
Mais - négligent - il dit
Paroles vilaines: un mot terrible
De son mal bec sortit!

Hélas! Elle dit, "Que c'est affreux!
Punir mon Trésor il faut
Dans le froid, "Frigo" pendant trois heures
A cause de son défaut."

L'oiseau enfin sortit plus sage,
Tout grelottant de froid,
Échevelé son beau plumage,
Yeux baissés, peureuse voix -

"Ce pauvre DINDON! Quel fut son tort?
Là…dans "Le Frigo"…je l'ai vu…
Lié…sans tête…gelé a mort…
Et toutes ses plumes perdues!"

Auntie Meg's Two Parrots

Auntie Meg acquires a second parrot to keep the first one company, thinking that a lady parrot might be a good influence. This, however, produces more problems.

Two parrots Auntie Meg possessed
And she did love them well.
In spite of this she was distressed,
For she could never tell

Which one the lady was - or dame -
And which one was the gent,
For both of them looked just the same
And had the same bird scent.

One day at last a thing occurred
Which meant she could not fail
To know without a doubt which bird
Was obviously the male.

One bird across the room did fly,
On th'other's perch did stop.
It had a twinkle in its eye
And gave a frisky hop.

Then for a kiss it gave a peck
And tried to give a cuddle,
But got, with wings around its neck,
Its feathers in a muddle.

It whispered then another word,
Another kiss it gave.
Meg said, "The male one is that bird,
For that's how men behave."

So that she always could decide
Between parrot he and she,
White ribbon round his neck she tied
To show that this was he.

He parrot thought 'twas meant to hurt
Because of what he'd done,
That he was punished as a flirt
Who'd had his bit of fun.

Envoi
The vicar called, dry, old, a scholar,
A man of dignity.
Around his neck a stiff white collar,
A celibate was he.

He parrot screamed with raucous laughter -
"White neckband I can see.
What girl have you been running after
And flirting with, like me?"

Pages 70 - 75 have the theme of, "It depends how you say it" or "How you hear it."

The Colonel

The Colonel was a dry old stick:
No sense of humour had he.
Sad to relate, he often felt sick
When crossing the great wide sea.

As he voyaged home on the sea so wide
On the port side was his berth,
While on the opposite starboard side
Was very old Lady McGirth.

Poor Colonel felt sick on this ocean so wide.
Thought he might perhaps improve
If across to the opposite starboard side
He somehow might make a move.

For back in his youth the Colonel had heard
Or read in a learnèd tome
That P - O - S - H, posh, this small word
Meant Port Out, Starboard Home.

"Have my place," said kind Lady McGirth,
"On the starboard side of the boat."
In exchange he gave the lady his berth,
Then emailed home this brief note -

Envoi
"Morning: Sickness bad as could be."
(Read aloud this caused great mirth.)
"Afternoon at about half past three
I to an old woman gave berth."

Pete's Granny

Pete's granny came with him to stay
As grannies often do,
And took the little lad one day
On a visit to the zoo.

To th'aviary they made their way
To see exotic birds.
Gran read their names, some hard to say
For they were Latin words.

When Pete had climbed up on the wall,
A better view to gain,
He lost his step and had a fall.
Then started to complain.

"My head hurts!" cried the little lad.
His granny felt his head.
She thought it did not seem too bad.
"We'll have it checked," she said.

The First Aid Post was very near.
The nurse gave Pete a hug,
Examined him, then said, "My dear,
You need pain-killing drug."

"Some tablets will your pain relieve
After your nasty fall.
We should have some, I do believe,
The Paracetemol."

Envoi
Then Peter's granny shook her head,
Surprised by nurse's words.
"If parrots eat "em all," she said,
"Then kill the wretched birds."

Young Jan
A sonnet

Young Jan to his homeland was flying back.
His flight took off: above the zoo soon turned.
Jan's dictionary was locked up in his pack
But he remembered many words he'd learned.
A baby - for example - this he knew
And zebra - animal striped black and white.
Take off - he'd heard folk say this as they flew.
These words proved useful on his homeward flight.
A zebra with her young he, looking down, espied,
And, keen to share with others this fair scene,
Turned t'wards th'old lady at his side,
Who at his words let out a dreadful scream.
In broken English he'd poured out each word:
"Take off - zebra - baby," the old lady heard.

The Two Motorists
A short ode

The bra to the top hat once said,
"I suggest you go on ahead.
I must wait here on my own
To give a lift to Auntie Joan."

As the Cat Heard It

"For Sunday lunch," I heard her say,
"I've invited Hattie."
"What for?" asked he in great dismay,
"She's become so catty."

"I know," said she. "Don't be unkind,
But understand the cause.
Hattie has trouble in her mind,
For she has many paws."

I heard and thought, "What will I see?"
How will this Hattie walk?
Upright or on her paws like me?
Which paw will hold her fork?"

I longed to see this sight so weird.
I am a curious cat!
But when this friend at last appeared
Everything fell quite flat.

No paws she had, but hands and feet.
To eat she used her hand.
She stood upright, my folks to greet.
I do not understand.

Introduction to an Ambiguous Marriage: In common English usage, to marry can mean either to officiate at a wedding or to take a person as husband or wife. Some languages avoid this ambiguity. I once said, "I am going to marry [person]" and my small niece said, "I thought you were married to Auntie Stella." This poem shows the lifelong result of this ambiguity.

An Ambiguous Marriage
A ballad

He was a curate aged twenty-four,
And she sixteen that day.
He said, as they stood beside the church door,
"I'll marry you here one day."
Now English ambiguous can be
And a perfect gentleman was he.

He said these words with a smile on his face
As they strolled to the old lych-gate.
She answered his words with a loving embrace
And a promise, "My darling I'll wait."
Now English etc.

He meant that one day her wedding he'ld take
To some man, her own Mr Right.
She assumed that one day his wife she would make,
And her heart was filled with delight.
Now English etc.

She told her mummy who told her dad
The loving proposal she'd heard.
With tears in their eyes they said they were glad,
For clergymen keep to their word.
Now English etc.

He felt more deeply committed,
When a diamond ring they bought.
She kissed him three times when 'twas fitted.
"I ought to say something," he thought.
Now English etc.

Relations and friends were invited.
Too late, he thought, to explain.
She was happy and all were excited.
Cancelling now would cause pain.
Now English etc.

He was a curate of twenty-seven
And she at nineteen was his bride.
She felt she'd already reached heaven,
As she heard his vows at her side.
Now English etc.

74

He was a Vicar of forty.
She loved the Vicarage life.
Parishioners all said that they thought he
Had chosen well for his wife.
Now English etc.

He was Archdeacon at fifty.
The clergy all said they were fine.
His Diocesan budget was thrifty:
She invited their wives in to dine.
Now English etc.

A Bishop now, expert at chairing
Committees and meetings galore.
Episcopal life she loved sharing.
Never called Synods a bore.
Now English etc.

In his Diocese all now admired him.
"Their children - all so well taught.".
"His wife has really inspired him."
Too late for truth, he now thought.
Now English etc.

He'd been a curate of twenty-four
And she a girl of sixteen.
Little he thought, as they stood by that door,
What his casual words might mean.
But English etc.

This ballad has two alternative endings

Either
Retirement came to lives well spent.
He thought, "She never need know
What 'marry you' really meant
In that year of long ago."
Now English etc.

Or
Retirement came to lives well spent.
Smiling his wife said, "My dear,
I knew quite well what 'marry' meant
On your lips that far off year.
But marry ambiguous can be,
And you were Mr Right for me."

Food is the theme in page 76 to 83.

Fifty Foods

We often have books and articles telling us what foods are good for our health. This poem is based on an article in *The Times* of 24th October 2016 that gave details of fifty foods to make one look younger and live longer.

Now Julie read in *The Times* one day
Fifty foods to keep old age at bay.
They would help to maintain youthful good looks.
Some we eat raw and others one cooks.
When Julie read a useful new thing
Heart and soul into this she would fling.
She decided the ageing process to beat,
All of these fifty foods she would eat.

"Celery and oysters, beef, pumpkin seeds
Are best if romantic love one needs.
I ate ten oysters a day - far too much in excess,
To spice up our marriage I must confess."
One day she wanted a hug and a kiss
Till her husband said, "Just give it a miss.
It's okay for young couples to be romantics.
At our age we need rest, not mad antics."

"Oily fish, sardines, tofu I now find
Help the memory, brain and the mind.
Instead of longing for romantic thrill
Of food for the mind I'll eat my fill."
But her husband whom she upset again,
Quoted Martial about a wife's brain -
"Sit non coniunx doctissima:
That's meant for you, Julia carissima."

"I've twice put my husband in a bad mood.
Tuna and onions will now be my food.
For my shape to be slim these foods are just right.
Soon he'll look at his wife with delight."
Julia ate too much of the food again
And became as thin as a bamboo cane.
He used her to tie up his runner beans.
Things never turn out quite as one means!

"I'm just at the age of menopause,
Which may some unpleasant signs now cause.
As flax seed is best to keep these away,
I'll put lots in my food every day."
A group of her friends discussed their hot flush.
This chatting came to a sudden hush.
For all of her friends were very upset
By Julie's claim, "Hot flush I don't get."

"For lovely thick hair to grow on one's head,
'Cucumber is best,' the article said.
To look really good I'll buy cucumber,
Of which I shall eat a very large number."
But too much cucumber caused her much harm.
As well as her head, each leg and each arm.
Her neck and her back were covered in hair.
She was put in the zoo and labelled "She Bear."

"Low cholesterol level keeps the heart fine.
To have a fine heart, drink a glass of red wine.
I did not see that the glass must be small,
Bought three bottles a day and drank them all."
After a party with a generous host
She drove right into a big lamp post.
The Magistrates' Court and her insurance agree
That "sake of my health" was a bad defence plea.

"Tomatoes and salmon keep skin young looking.
Each day I'll put loads of these in my cooking.
Miso paste on each dish I will sprinkle
On my youthful face there won't be one wrinkle."
With a very smooth skin like a pre-adolescent
To watch an adult film our Julie then went.
The cashier looked at her baby-smooth skin
And said, "Sorry dear, can't let you in."

"To help the heart and blood circulation
(Once again I forgot moderation)
The article said that garlic is best,
So I served plenty to each dinner guest."
But our Classics Master quoted Horatius
About, "Cicutis allium nocentius
Quid hoc veneni saevit in praecordiis
In future we'll give your dinners a miss."

"So much has gone wrong, I'm feeling contrite,
Lots of walnuts and oats will put matters right.
They're energy foods so I'll never get tired,
But work very hard, like a woman inspired."
With her energy level on the increase
Our Julie gave no one a moment of peace.
In despair her husband called out, yawning,
"Do come to bed, it's three in the morning."

"Now I'll try to relax. This time I won't fail.
This needs broccoli, turkey and kale.
I'll calm down if I eat lots of this stuff.
(Again I ate far more than enough)."
Julie fell asleep in the bath at night.
Asleep when letters she ought to write,
Asleep in church when vicar was preaching,
Asleep at school instead of teaching.

"I've tried all these foods but I've failed to beat
The ageing process by foods which I eat.
For in spite of all my best endeavour
I know I can't be young forever.
I realise I've made an awful mess
By eating fifty foods to such excess.
My motto was, but with too zealous a touch,
Of a good thing one can't have too much."

A little bit of what you fancy does you good
Is her motto now when buying food.
When shopping she has a good long think
And buys her favourite food and drink.
In her kitchen at home she happily sighs,
Eats fatty bacon and eggs which she fries.
Enjoys a big burger with plenty of chips
And FIFTY FOODS into pieces she rips.

Latin quotations

Sit non doctissima coniunx
A wife should not be too learnèd.
Martial. Epigrams. 2:90

Cicutis allium nocentius
Garlic more deadly than hemlock.

Quid hoc veneni saevit in praecordiis?
What is this poison that rages in my stomach?
Horace: Epode 3. His patron had served garlic at dinner.

Fiona's Birthday Dinner

Fiona Smythe-Jones was very good-looking,
Loved to dress up and was proud of her cooking.
Her friends all considered her dinners the best.
Each one was delighted to come as her guest.

For her birthday she planned a feast to prepare
And invited twelve guests her dinner to share.
The starter was, "Fiona's Own Special Dish."
The main course - "Salmon Mousse with Fiona's Garnish."

Her guests thought the starter a lovely surprise.
Fiona was proud to be praised to the skies.
She went to the kitchen to bring in the Mousse,
Found a piece had been eaten by naughty young puss.

Clever Fiona, not to be beaten,
Smoothed over the place where pussy had eaten.
Her guests ate the mousse and each of them said
That never before had they been so well fed.

Outside stepped Fiona, for fresh air a breath
And there she saw poor pussy, stretched right out in death.
"The fish must be poisoned," she wanted to cry.
Unless she did something, her guests would all die.

Fiona went back and this sad tale confessed.
She felt so ashamed in the eyes of each guest.
She rang up the hospital, told A and E,
Who said, "Bring them here, as quick as can be."

Twelve guests must then leave the dessert she'd prepared
And rush to the hospital, all feeling scared.
All had stomach pumps, a painful proceeding.
Some loudly complained of internal bleeding.

All twelve of her guests, with a sharp stomach pain,
Said, "Eat at Fiona's? No! Never again!"
All twelve of her guests, from the pump feeling sore,
Cried, "Fiona's dinners? No! Never! No more!"

Fiona felt sad, in vain all her labour.
She found by the door a note from her neighbour -
"You'll find a body stretched out on the mat.
I'm sorry I ran over and killed your poor cat."

The Cannibal poems on the next two pages have been included in the
Food section. Like several of these verses they began their lives as
harmless little jokes. Some may think that with a reference to mother-in-
law, and possibly a racist suggestion, that they are politically incorrect
and written, "aegro in corde" (with a sick mind). In defence I can say
that the first one has been used in a sermon to show the different
meanings of love.

The Cannibals' Feast
A ballad

Some cannibals in the jungle's shade
Were planning a special feast.
The food was cooking, the places laid
For both greatest and for least.

All were rejoicing in dance and song.
Clapping hands and stamping feet.
All, all, were happy the whole day long
With thoughts of the juicy meat.

All, all, save one who sat on his own.
In the joys he took no part.
His gloomy face as he sat alone
Revealed a very sad heart.

This cannibal brave who shed a tear
Was a young man, newly wed.
A wise old cannibal, drawing near,
Took his hand and gently said,

"Dear boy, you take no part in our song.
Your sadness cannot feel nice.
Open your heart and tell me what's wrong.
I'm old and can give good advice."

The young man replied, "My wife, like a dove,
Is gentle, soft and refined.
But mother-in-law I cannot love.
She's hard and tough I shall find."

Envoi
The wise one, versed in the married state,
Gave a gentle smile and said,
"Then leave her on the side of the plate
And eat extra chips instead."

Another Cannibal Feast: *A ballad*
Two explorers, sad to say,
In the jungle lost their way,
By some cannibals were found,
Carried off, both tightly bound.

Great Chief sat in kingly state
Told the couple of their fate.
"Your flesh looks like juicy meat,
Which at dinner we shall eat.

Your skulls will then my hut adorn
Or as trophies will be worn.
Useful bones my wife employs,
Kitchen tools or children's toys.

For your skins good use I'll find.
New canoes I have in mind.
Your skins will, when shaped and dried,
Form the bottom and the side.

Though we are a warrior race.
I will grant a special grace.
You may have, before you're killed
Any final wish fulfilled."

Came an answer, clear and quick.
"Please," a captive said, "Just prick
Our skins all over with a fork.
We shall need no further talk."

The other captive to his friend
Whispered, "What a way to end.
Pricking will cause us pain I fear.
Why not ask for fags or beer?"

Envoi
"My last wish," replied his mate,
"Will cause the Chief a gloomy fate.
With these pinprick holes, I think,
Chief's canoe is sure to sink."

Pages 84 - 93 have an educational theme on training the young. As well as the main items, a few "Question and Answer Howlers" are scattered around. The oddest one that I heard was in a test after I had included Joshua and the Capture of Jericho in the lessons. A pupil's essay on Joshua and Jericho began, "Joshua and Jericho were very good friends..." and gave a touching account of their friendship. Unfortunately it was not a test on creative writing.

The Primary School Photograph
A sonnet

Teacher was showing a school photograph,
Hoping that parents would buy one to own.
She said to the children, "Now you may laugh.
One day into adults you will have all grown.
And then perhaps you'll be mummies and dads,
Who'll say, 'This is me thirty years ago.'
You can point out here the young girls and lads,
And say what they do as their photo you show -
'This one's a nurse - he now drives a train.
This one's a farmer. My friend is this one.
Maybe this one runs a hotel in Spain!'
You'll point them all out, so won't that be fun!"
"I'll point you out, Miss," a dear laddie said,
"And say, 'That's our teacher: now she is dead.'"

Q. People and places. Who can say
What was Salome famous for?
A. She was a girl who danced one day
Right in front of Harrods store.

The Missing Pencils

"Please miss, I ain't got no pencil," called out the little lad.
Teacher tried to correct him because his grammar was bad.
So she said,
"I have no pencil,
You have no pencil,
He / she has no pencil,
We have no pencil,
You have no pencil,
They have no pencil."
She thought she'd explained "to have no" by this careful conjugation,
But it only left the little lad a sense of deep frustration.
So he said,
"If you and all them other kids ain't got no pencils same as me,
Then I'ld like to know where on earth can all the flippin' pencils be."

Q. Solomon a thousand wives had wed.
Why did this cause trouble?
A. He needed to have a giant bed,
But the largest size was double.

Q. Write a sentence to make its meaning clear
Where "meander" does appear.
A. Mum met me at the school bus stop
Then me and 'er went off to shop.

The Missing Spoon or The Cookery Lesson

A schoolgirl learning how to cook
Was puzzling in her head,
So with a very puzzled look
She to her teacher said -

"In this School Cookery Book I read,
To make a Christmas cake,
Of one ingredient that you need,
A level teaspoon take.

I searched each box, I searched each drawer,
I hunted all around,
But though I see teaspoons galore,
No level teaspoon found."

Q. Oil pollution kills life in sea and soil.
Give examples that you've seen or read.
A. Mum opened a tin of sardines in oil,
And all the fish inside were dead.

Q. What was the role in history
Of an island called Capri?
A. Capri has lots of visitors.
One called Gracie had a fling
In a field of aspidistras
With Tiberius, a king.

Some clerihews on training the young.

On Beating

1st Century BC
Orbilius has won lasting fame
With The Beater as his second name.
In his school, wrote Quintus Flaccus,
He used to teach but also wack us.

19th Century AD
John Keate, the Head of Eton,
Found a group of boys waiting and had them all beaten.
Afterwards one said, "But sir we came for preparation.
We're your class of confirmation."

Schoolmasters

1st Century AD
Celadus and Palemon worked hard all day
As teachers with very little pay.
The parents did not respect them,
Juvenal said, as gentlemen.

19th Century AD
Thomas Arnold, Rugby's head, maintained
That his teaching staff should be ordained,
For in England everyone knows that a clergyman
Has the profession of a gentleman.

Notes
Orbilius: Horace. Epistles 2: 1: 70
John Keate: Headmaster of Eton. Famous for flogging.
Celadus and Palemon: Juvenal Satire VII: 215
Thomas Arnold: Letter of 19th March 1839
…the profession of a schoolmaster in society…owes the rank which it holds to its connexion with the profession of a clergyman, for that is acknowledged universally in England to be the profession of a gentleman.

Tom's First Words
A ballad

New baby Tom was fit and well.
So ev'rything seemed right.
His loving parents' hearts did swell
With pride and with delight.

But by the end of Tom's first years
He'd not said "Mum" or "Dad."
His parents, feeling this was queer,
Began to feel quite sad.

Another year had slipped away.
Tom no word had spoken.
The hearts that once were proud and gay
Now were almost broken.

Another birthday came - Tom's third -
He was still fit and well.
Yet still his parents had not heard
That Tom had things to tell.

Now Tom was not a naughty boy.
He did as he was taught.
But spoke no word of grief or joy.
His parents were distraught.

At four Tom seemed a happy child.
With other boys did play.
Yet though he often laughed and smiled
No sentence did he say.

His parents read a parents' book
To find what it could teach.
To doctors, clinics Tom they took
And therapists for speech.

These all advised, gave Tom a test,
But none of them could find
(Although they did their very best)
Why Tom was so behind.

He had not spoken at five years
His parents lost all hope.
"At school," they asked with many tears,
"How will poor Tommy cope?"

Then suddenly Tom's silence broke
At the dinner table,
There the first thing of which he spoke,
'Twas on a soup tin's label!

"This soup has such a dreadful taste
The label must be phoney.
It smells like rubbish from the waste,
Not like minestrone."

His parents' hearts were full of joy
Though hurt by Tom's rude word.
"Oh why are these, our darling boy,
Your first words that we've heard?"

Envoi
"Life was fine," the boy replied,
"With all that I desired.
Until this awful soup I tried,
No speeches were required."

Perhaps we all know people who never speak except to complain!

Q. Where do you find mangoes?
Just give the country's name.
A. Man goes where woman goes.
Mum says they're all the same.

Q. Next week - courgette - the paper said:
Its use for us explain.
A. It is a special kind of bed
You sleep in on a train.

A Christmas Present for Teacher

St Hilda's was a happy school
For those who learnt and those who taught.
Because Miss Roberts was so cool
Each girl a Christmas present brought.

Jill's father kept a butchers' shop.
Jill gave a turkey, plump and fine.
Miss Roberts gave a joyful hop
And planned whom she would ask to dine.

Sue's dad a bakery did run.
Sue gave a great big Christmas cake.
Miss Roberts said, "Oh thanks! What fun!
Now I shall have no need to bake."

Sal's mum a boutique owned - très chic -
So Sally gave a lovely skirt.
Miss Roberts said, "I'll look so sleek
That all the men will want to flirt."

Joan had a publican for dad,
The landlord of the Hen and Fox.
Miss Roberts felt so very glad
For Joan's gift was a great big box.

Miss Roberts guessed it must be drink.
Joan's dad would send no other thing.
She smiled with joy and said, "I think
My party will go with a swing!"

Joan said, "Three guesses!" She must try
To find out what the box contained
Miss Roberts saw with eagle eye
Some liquid from the box had drained.

She thought, "There is a broken flask
Or from Champagne a cork has popped.
Of course I'll guess - no need to ask."
And once again with joy she hopped.

She filled a glass and without haste
Drank the liquid clear and fine.
It had a strange exotic taste.
Her first guess was Champagne or wine.

First guess was wrong. She could guess twice.
She filled and drank, then said, "It's beer."
Still wrong, although it tasted nice.
Her third guess - grog - still wrong I fear.

At last Joan said, with laugh so bold,
"It is not wine, nor beer, nor grog.
I will the mystery unfold -
This box contains - a puppy dog!"

The Cubs visit the Race Course
A Ballad

The cubs' theme was, "Life of a Horse."
To badge awards this led.
They planned to attend a big race course
With Akela at their head.

She told them, "Just wear your normal dress
To go and watch the race.
Cubs at the course may cause distress
Although it's no disgrace."

This gave an idea to a cub called Bert.
"Dress like jockeys," he said.
"With colours on our cap and shirt,
Blue, scarlet, yellow, red."

At the course they went
To use the W.C. -
A gutter long, in canvas tent,
Where one could stand and wee.

But soon the cubs came with a cry
And made an awful fuss -
"Akela! Akela! It's far too high."
"It's out of reach for us."

Puzzled, Akela thought, "Oh dear.
I ought to be prepared.
This calls for action bold, I fear."
So this is what she dared -

Although she had a woman's looks
Akela was quite strong.
Although her plan was in no books,
She felt it was not wrong.

Though she a lady was, not gent.
The rules she did defy.
Boldly she entered the gentlemen's tent
To lift each cub on high.

One cub she lifted up for a wee,
Then gave a sudden shout -
"Oh, you're far too heavy for me.
You ought to be a scout."

Envoi
"Thanks love, for that," this lad replied,
"But scouts are not for me.
I'm the jockey who's due to ride
The race at half-part three."

After the education section we move onto more advanced learning.
Pages 94 - 105 contain verses on the theme of Classical Civilisation.

We begin with

The Trojan War: Its causes and sequel in the Founding of Rome, told in limericks

Queen Hecuba said, "How I hate all
My dreams after ante-natal.
From the clinic I come
An expectant young mum
And dream that my babe will prove fatal."

"There's our teenage daughter Cassandra.
Perhaps her trouble is glandular.
Her hair looks a sight,
She cries 'Woe!' day and night.
I simply don't understand her."

A lovely nymph called Oenone
Lived in the woods feeling lonely.
While she sat on Mount Ida
Paris sat down beside her
And spoke words of love (which proved phoney).

Thetis, when she took Peleus as mate,
Said, "Come, gods and goddesses, celebrate!"
On the wedding guest list
Just one name was missed -
Goddess of Discord, whose presence would grate.

94

The spiteful Eris thought it a slight
When she did not receive an invite.
So she caused a wide rift
With the apple, her gift,
On which "To the Fairest Goddess" she did write.

The gods planned a beauty contest,
And three soon defeated the rest.
The finalist of three
Miss Olympus would be.
But who would be judge of the best?

Wily Zeus said, "I'm not such an ass
As to be judge of the prettiest lass.
The two who weren't best
Would give me no rest.
I'll tell Paris to solve this impasse."

When the contest on Ida took place
Each girl came with a smile on her face,
With a meaningful nudge
And a smile for the judge,
But in private their words had no grace.

Thought the wise intellectual Athene
"I'm sure to win when he sees me.
I don't want to sound catty
But Aphrodite's a fatty,
And Hera's brain, unlike mine, is too teeny."

Hera thought, "If Miss Olympus I can't be
Aphrodite won't defeat me.
Against her son I'll rage.
Called Juno I'll wage
Bitter war by hand and by sea."

The goddess of love, Aphrodite,
Thought, "Surely Paris won't slight me,
I know I can't fail.
At the January sale
I bought this pink see-through nightie."

Athene complained, "Your cheating's unfair.
Take off that magical thing that you wear."
Venus agreed, "I'll do that
If you take off your hat."
Paris, grinning, said, "All three must be bare."

Hera whispered to Paris, "A king!
Great power and prestige that will bring!
That's what you will be
If you just vote for me."
Paris thought, "That sounds a good thing."

Athene promised, "Much blood you will shed,
As a fighter whom all men will dread,
Feared and renowned
If Miss Olympus I'm crowned."
"It's hard to choose," to himself Paris said.

Cuddling close, Aphrodite murmured, "Dear lad,
The world's loveliest girl drives men mad.
I'll give her as your bride
To live close by your side."
Paris thought, "That's the best offer I've had."

Of course Aphrodite came first.
The others resentment both nursed.
Paris sailed with great joy.
Brought back Helen to Troy.
Her husband was cross: Troy was cursed.

Priam said, "Your actions betray us.
You've angered King Menelaus.
I'm told he has heard
You've stolen his bird,
And he's on his way to repay us."

Helen said, "Oh why did you say
You loved me and dragged me away?
Now I can't go exploring
And it's terribly boring
Stuck here in the city all day."

Though she thought inside was a bore,
Outside was blood with red gore.
Hector and Achilles,
A pair of big sillies,
Said, "Let's give it a name - Trojan War."

Replied Paris to Helen, "'Tisn't right
For me not to go out and fight,
For I started this fray
When I took you away -
And there's not much on telly tonight."

So out Paris went. Sitting duck,
Whom Philoctetes' arrow struck.
Oenone, nymph betrayed,
Refused his wound to aid,
Said, "Sorry Paris, rotten luck!"

When the Greeks could not win by brute force,
Epeios cried, "I gotta horse!
Put your bets on this nag;
We'll all share the swag."
You all know what happened of course.

Laocoon cried, "Please take note:
For later ages here's a good quote -
Greeks give one a scare
When their gifts they bear."
Alas! Serpents caught the poor man's throat.

Aeneas sailed away from this scene.
Ubi Troia fuit - Troy was a has-been
With his young lad
And frail old dad,
Harassed by heaven's vexed queen.

Thus had Aeneas his journey begun
(Remember he was Venus' son).
So when things went wrong
Venus popped along.
It helps to have a goddess as mum.

Harassed by Juno's efforts to scare him
He passed per tot discrimina rerum.
(Though translating may bore
That means "hazards galore")
With his brave band of heroes to share them.

In th'underworld he faced alone
Dog Cerberus with his fierce savage groan,
For the angry dog thought
"A useless bough he's brought,
When I wanted a nice tasty bone."

So winning great honour and fame
To Latium at last Aeneas came,
Where 'twas decreed by Fate
He should found a new state
With Pius tacked on to his name.

Even when he left Dido dementem
He claimed iussa deum had sent him.
To conclude we read that
Tantae molis erat
Romanam condere gentem.

Iusse deum - orders of the gods. Virgil Aeneid 6:461
Tantae molis erat Romanam condere getem. Virgil. Aeneid 1: 33,34

Classical Clerihews

Here are four pages of clerihews, that particularly English form of biography, taken from history, literature and mythology, in alphabetical order.

The hunter **Actaeon**
Happened to see Artemis without her clothes on.
For this breach of etiquette beyond permitted bounds
He was turned into a stag and killed by his own hounds.

Augustus is the name each century ALWAYS knows,
At first because he overcame all foes.
In horticulture he has a more peaceful cause for fame
As Semper Augustus was an expensive seventeenth century tulip's name.

Gaius Julius Caesar
Sometimes had a seizure.
It is not surprising that an Italian bon viveur had fits
On first tasting - in 55BC - the food of the Brits.

The nymph **Calypso** tried to misbehave
With stranded Ulysses inside her cave.
When he sailed away, the nymph in desperation
Sang a West Indian song with rhythm of syncopation.

Celsus gave us moderns cause to bless
Opticians, eye-surgeons and the N H S.
When in de Medicina Book VII he described the gruesome facts
Of an ancient eye operation for cataracts.

To senate and people said **Cicero, Marcus Tullius,**
"Catiline is trying to bully us."
So that all ages his victory should note
"O fortunatam natam me consule Romam," he wrote.

The emperor **Claudius** was really very odd
Though after his death people thought he was a god.
If Latin you cannot read
Robert Graves will give you all the details that you need.

Pulcher Publius Clodius
Invading the Rites of the Bone Dea was not pulcher but odious.
I felt it was just as sinister
When I was the only male cleric at the Institution of a lady minister.

Though **Crassus** had a large amount of money,
He laughed only once, so his life did not seem funny.
This is not surprising since he was a subordinate
To Caeser and Pompey in the First Triumvirate.

Dido, Queen of Cathage, lost all sense of shame
When her heart was set on fire by love's fierce flame.
Later her body was consumed by fire
On her funeral pyre.

"Maxime!" "Verracuse!" perhaps parents of little **Fabius** used to say.
"Hurry up!" "Get a move on!" "Be quick!" "Don't delay!"
All parents say this, but these did not know
That their son would be famous for saving Rome cunctando.

Helen, Zeus' and Leda's daughter,
Caused ten years of war, pain and slaughter.
Leaving Troy in flames and a heap of rubble,
Just said to Menelaus, "Sorry if I caused a spot of trouble."

Horace, Quintus Flaccus,
Adored the god of wine, old Bacchus.
If the garlic that Maecenas gave him had really been venemous
He could not have lived to write a monumentum aere perennius.

Augustus' granddaughter **Julia**
Led a lifestyle that was peculiar.
She caused her grandad distress
When she often featured in Rome's tabloid press.

Titus **Livius,** to proclaim Rome's glory,
Wrote CXLII books of her story,
From the founding of the City.
But CVII were lost, which is a pity.

Lucretius thought it was not quite nice
For Agamemnon to offer his daughter in sacrifice.
So that we should not behave in this fashion
He wrote a long poem about Void and the Atom.

Old **Menoetes** had a nasty shock
When he was thrown into the sea and climbed on a rock.
Sitting there in dripping clothes, the poor man's grief
Gave th'Aeneid its only laughs and light relief.

The emperor **Nero,** who killed many of Rome's nobility.
In a fit of downward social mobility
Sang like a pop star with elation,
Then killed his aunt who had constipation.

The poet **Ovid**
Long before Covid
Was sent a long way from Rome in isolation
Where he wrote Tristia, a lamentation.

Penelope ("Just call me Penny")
Found it hard to choose a suitor from so many.
Her problem was solved when all were killed by Odysseus,
Who returned after twenty years to claim his missus.

In his plays Titus Meacus **Plautus**
Much about the seamy side of Roman life he taught us,
Misers, grumpy old men, young men with love life in a mess,
Cunning slaves, pimps, courtesans and their procuress.

Gaius **Suetonius** Tranquillus
Told naughty tales that will thrill us,
About people, like Nero, who sang on Rome's stages
And murdered their mother and committed other outrages.

Tiberius was lustful like an old goat
Of his decadent island life Suetonius wrote.
Because goat is caper in translation
Capri was the island's designation.

Cicero's slave-secretary **Tiro**
Probably had a sort of biro,
So that when Cicero said something grand
He wrote it down in his own short hand.

It is not easy to translate humour from one language to another. As regards short verses this difficulty is increased by the fact that Latin does not use rhyme, which English does. Martial is known for his epigrams. English humour often is expressed by Limericks or Clerihews. Four of these are translated here. On this page two are about doctors, regarding whom Romans were not always flattering. I showed the first to a doctor who had apologised for having cold hands.

Languebam: sed tu comitatus protinus ad me
venisti centum, Symache, discipulis.
Centum me tetigere manus aquilone gelatae:
non habui febum, Symache, nunc habeo (5:9)

Doctor Symachus, when I had a slight chill,
You came and showed a hundred students your skill.
Cold hands gave a stroke,
Frozen fingers a poke.
"Slight chill," turned to fever made me ill.

The following is even more cynical -
Nuper erat medicus, nunc est vispillo Diaulus:
quod vispillo fecit, fecerat et medicus (1:47)

There was a doctor, Diaulus by name,
Who a funeral director became.
Nothing's changed, people said.
He now buries the dead,
So his profession remains just the same.

Omnes aut vetulas habes amicas,
aut turpes vetulisque foediores.
Has ducis comies trahisque tecum
per convivia, porticus, theatra.
Sic formosa, Fabula, sic puella es. (8:79)

You, Fabula, take old hags to share each treat,
And walk with ugly girls along the street,
Friends who lack a single grace,
Girls without a pretty face.
Why? Next to them, you're charming, young and sweet.

Petit Getnellus nuptias Maronillae
et cupit et instat et precatur et donat.
Adeone pulchra est? Immo foedius nil est.
Quid ergo in illa petitur et placet? Tussit. (1:10)

A fairly free translation -
Young Getnellus wooed in Rome's city
Marinolla, a girl far from pretty.
He though her bad cough
Would soon carry her off
And he'd got what's left in the kitty.

Similarly -
Nubere Paula cupit nobis, ego ducere Paulam
nolo: anus est: vellem. si magis esset anus (10:8)

When Paula wanted me to wed,
She's much too old for me. I said.
If she had been much older still,
Of course I would have said, "I will."

Holy Laughter

There is much material for gentle amusement in the life of the church, so pages 106 - 131 are an ecclesiastical section. However, to make a link with the preceding section, the first two pages have a classical aspect.

The Church of England now allows women to be consecrated as bishops. Here we make a link with a quotation from Virgil -

et tunicae manicas et habent redimicula mitrae,
o vere Phrygiae, neque enim Phryges. Aeneid 9:616

Your tunics have sleeves and your mitres have ribbons.
You are certainly Phrygian women, not men.

As a limerick -
To be a bishop a lady felt led
For in Aeneid Book 9 she had read
That a beautiful mitre
Is no sign of a fighter,
But designed for a lady's fair head.

In some churches, sober traditional organ worship has been replaced by more excitable styles. Here we have a link with a long quotation from Catullus about the young man Attis and frenzied worship -

Super alta vectus Attis celeri rate maria...
stimulatus ibi furenti rabie...
...cepit manibus leve tympanum...
ubi cymbalum sonat vox, ubi tympana reboant,
tibicem ubi canat Phryx
curvo grave calamo
Catullus 63

Attis was carried over the deep seas by his swift boat.
...took up the light timbrel,
where the noise of timbrels sounds, where timbrels echo,
where the Phygian flute player blows a deep note on the curved reed.

As a limerick -
Attis in frenzy took a tympanum,
Calamus and the vox cymbalum.
Thus some churches today
Instead of organs like to play
Guitars and the beating drum.

The classical theme continues with a question of pronouncing Latin. V said as V or W has varied in England over the years. Our school had a French assistant who spoke Latin with a French accent. I heard of a Latin speaking contest won by pretty seventeen-year-old girls who put on an Italian accent. This sonnet was written after a discussion with our organist when rehearsing a musical setting of the Gloria in Latin

Sonnet to a Beautiful Lady who is Badly Dressed by her Friends

O GLORIA! Thou art most welcome here
If dressed in EXCELSIS (said with Kay).
But how much pain it gives my learnèd ear
To listen while the choir EGGSHELLSIS say.
And GRATIAS, when said with a Tee,
Is to my ears a gratifying word.
Then AGIMUS should have a good hard G
(In Latin Jay is never, never heard).
Your Joy KAELESTIS we all mortals share
(In Latin CH we never, never find).
This strange unclassic dress you're told to wear
From classic grace has sadly much declined.
Dear GLORIA! when next you come again
Please wear your classic dress to spare my pain.

The Seduction and Gentrification of Carol
A ballad

I was a simple country girl
And Carol was my name.
My hair once had a natural curl
Which none had tried to tame.

My lips had still their natural shade
And not a brighter hue,
My nails as Mother Nature made,
Not scarlet or bright blue.

The songs we sang were all home-grown
As Christmastide came round.
Things such as descant were unknown,
But simple country sound.

Church gallery held our rustic choir
As in Hardy's novel
We sang in Big House for the squire
Or in poor folks' hovel.

Then to our village came one day
A man from London town.
He heard the simple tunes we play,
He looked me up and down.

He said my simple country face
In its way was pretty,
But took me from my country place
Away to London city.

Many things he taught me there
That turned my simple head.
I learnt to tie my flowing hair,
My nails I painted red.

This musical arranger, he
(Such was his profession)
To change my style, oft gave to me
A special singing lesson.

I used to be a simple country girl called Carol!

My natural voice he tried to tame,
I learned to paint my lips.
My favourite drink became
                              Champagne
In dainty little sips.

And now that I am so refined
With loss of simple looks,
My present life all folk can find
In our church choir's new books.

Envoi
So as my life's been rearranged
With descants and such things,
I think my name should now be
                              changed
In places where one sings.

A simple girl with simple name,
Carol was just fine;
Now I've become a splendid dame
Please call me Carolyne.

Forward to 2099

A sonnet

Page 106 refers to the consecration of women bishops. Before that the Church of England authorised the ordination of women as priests. In a recent year it was reported that more women than men had been ordained. This inspired the following sonnet.

Now in this year of Twenty Ninety-Nine
We Anglicans are very close to splitting,
For some there are who say it would be fine
And the practice would be very fitting
If we could extend priests' ordination
To men, who from the priesthood are kept out,
But others say 'twould be an innovation,
We have to right, tradition old to flout.
Then while they argue much, sometimes with rage
Whether with men the priesthood should be shared,
Up popped an ancient cleric, bent with age,
"Men once were priests," his croaking voice declared.
"I am the proof, for I am still alive
And was ordained a priest in Nineteen Fifty-Five."

A look at other aspects of modern church life.

The Charismatic Movement
From the second half of the twentieth century, one aspect of the charismatic movement was speaking in tongues, ecstatically uttering words in an unknown language -

There was a young Charismatic
Whose speech was extremely ecstatic,
He could say a new word
Which no one had heard,
So his Scrabble score was fantastic.

All Age Worship
Here the sermon (or "talk") is intended for people of all ages. As the following three pages show this is not easy.

One aspect of this is…

Messy Church, when all kinds of activities take place with paper, crayons etc. The word messy can confuse the foreign visitor.
Madame parlait anglais très peu.
Elle pensa, "La Messe à dix heures."
Elle est venu mais dit,
"Quelle étrange liturgie.
Ce rite modern - c'est affreux!"

All-Age Worship at the Parish Church

"All-age worship is the thing,"
The vicar said. "It's what we need.
<u>Together</u> we worship, pray and sing."
The PCC? They all agreed.

A start was made on Sunday week.
The vicar carefully had planned
For young and old some words to speak
In terms that <u>all</u> would understand.

That priest was eager to expound
That though the church has different parts,
As one we are together bound
By mutual love within our hearts.

"Each person has a special skill
For all some special gift possess.
So all their given roles fulfil.
None are worth more and none worth less."

"Think of body," vicar said.
He spoke at length to make things clear.
"Think of the things upon your head.
To help you listen is the ear."

"To help enjoy a tasty sweet
We have a tongue. Our lips can talk.
Then lower down we have two feet
To help us run and sometimes walk."

He spoke with care the words he should.
He was a man of ready tongue.
"At last," he thought, "I'm understood
Both by the old and by the young."

"Though each one has a different task,
They'll see we are together bound.
So now a question I will ask.
Their answers will be quite profound."

"Now we, the church, have eyes, feet, hands,
Joined in one body by some link.
What is this link? Who understands?
Stand up and say: What do you think?"

"Spirit of love is the tie that binds,"
The vicar hoped some child would say.
But he forgot that children's minds
Do not work this abstract way.

Up stood a thoughtful eight-year-old,
Sure of himself, he gave a grin.
He made his answer firm and bold.
"I know. Of course it is our skin."

On similar lines

To teach the young the vicar said,
"To help us run we have our feet.
A nose to smell the flowers so sweet."

A lad replied with shaking head,
"The bit that runs - my dirty nose.
The bit that smells - my feet and toes."

A similar misunderstanding occurs in

The Lost Sheep
A ballad

Rev'd John as parish priest once went
To sheep country up North.
With children there with good intent
The priest was holding forth.

The Lost Sheep Parable he read
And planned its truth t'expound.
But to the children first he said,
(wanting answers profound),

"When ninety-nine were safe behind
The fence that would them keep,
Why did the shepherd go to find
One solitary lost sheep?"

Comparing with the ninety-nine
The search for one lost sheep,
He hoped to hear of love divine
And saving grace so deep.

They spoke together, one by one,
Trying to understand,
Until one boy, a farmer's son,
Smiled and put up his hand.

Envoi
The vicar's heart was oh so glad!
His soul was lifted up.
"That one lost sheep," answered the lad,
Happen it were t'tup."

Clergy may have a similar experience with adults as well as with children. Many have probably been brought down to earth in this way.

Marriage Preparation with the Vicar

For each wedding celebration
The vicar took great care,
Having talks of preparation
With each new happy pair.

He at length to them expounded
The nature of married life,
So that firmly might be grounded
The estate of man and wife.

"Our human marriage is a sign
Through which deep truths are meant,
An image of the love divine
Known as a sacrament."

At last he asked the happy pair
If questions they had found
Or whether they would like to share
Comments and thoughts profound.

Hope made the vicar's breast rejoice,
Because up spoke the bride.
Who in a very anxious voice
To his request replied.

"There is one very special thing
That I for sure must know.
Will you permit the guests we bring
Confetti here to throw?"

Since the Reformation there have been "Parties" in the Church of England. Once called "High," "Low" or "Broad," now more often "Catholic," "Evangelical," sometimes prefixed with "Liberal." I have seen the prefix "gently" (never "fiercely"). However, "party" is a word with several meanings. Here the ambiguity leads to lifelong consequences, as with An Ambiguous Marriage on page 74.

The Ballad of the Non-Party Cleric

This is the tale of one called Joe
An ordinand was he.
His vicar - Guy - not High nor Low
Was simply C of E.

The vicar was Joe's mentor wise
Whose word did Joe believe.
Joe tried to follow his advice
In ways that were naïve.

To this young man the vicar said,
"Dear boy, take it from me,
If you want as priest to get ahead,
A party man don't be."

So at Oxford Joe all parties feared
And none did he attend.
Since all the girls thought Joe was weird,
Poor Joe had no girlfriend.

Joe next, three years at Oxford spent,
His final course began.
To clergy training college went,
A firm non-party man.

A party was, sedate affair,
Held when a bishop came.
Our hero, since he was not there,
"Joe Puritan" became.

When Joe a deacon then was made
With welcome party planned,
Joe said, "Can't come, I am afraid,
But hope you'll understand."

Parents called Joe, now priest, a shirk
At parties held that year.
Although in charge of children's work
Rev'd Joe did not appear.

As Vicar he kept well away
When parties were arranged.
Some in his church were heard to cry,
"A kind man, but deranged."

Though to draw Joe out, the M U tried
Coaxing him and kissing,
In their party at each Christmastide,
Joe was always missing.

When fifty years had passed away
Joe to himself then said,
"No party man, I never play
But have not got ahead."

Joe heard at last, in deep distress,
His mentor priest was dead.
His obituary was in the press,
And this is what Joe read,

"No party could claim Father Guy,
No party man was he.
No party low, no party high,
But simply C of E."

Joe read these words again, surprised,
To grasp their full intent.
Alas! Too late he realised
What Father Guy had meant.

Joe thought of parties missed in youth
And through long wasted years.
He thought, "If I'd but known the truth…"
Then poured forth copious tears.

Joe thought at last, "'Tis not too late.
The past can't be undone,
But future years can compensate
For my lost years of fun."

Envoi
A home for clergy who retire
Has residents who say,
"One strange old priest here does desire
A party every day."

Postscript
The doctor affirmed,
"I'm very concerned,
For when I did yesterday's clergy home round
A fresh new case of Grand Mal I have found."

Rev'd Joe replied,
"I'm very surprised
And upset by the words that you say
For the case I ordered was Grand Marnier."

Regarding clergy careers, it was recently suggested that there should
be a list of about three hundred clergy suitable for senior posts. For this
we have invented Freddie, the church's talent scout, on the next page.

The Ballad of Freddie, the Church's Talent Scout

Now Freddie is a talent scout
Who writes marks in his book.
So Freddie ev'ry day sets out.
For talent he must look.

His dad judged at the village shows,
Things like a Brussels sprout,
So Fred the marking system knows,
Which helps a talent scout.

His dad had judged with thought and care
Taste, colour, shape and size,
For each gave ticks, and did declare
Which sprout had won a prize.

Right from the start Fred makes a list
Of all points essential
And takes great care he has not missed
Each ordinand's potential.

One ordinand serves well at Mass
With skilful ring of bell.
One who has camped with men like Bash
Already preaches well.

At seminars Fred lies concealed
To hear what each one said.
Then so their minds might be revealed
Each essay he has read.

Then when each one a title gets,
Some posts are not the same,
Fred the training incumbent vets,
Gives tick for well-known name.

So when each one's ordained as priest,
Already there's a score
Of Freddie's ticks, for some have least
And some have many more.

When one stands up to preach The Word
And in the church espies
A stranger noting all he's heard -
That's Freddie in disguise.

Then when at last all can rejoice
In parish of their own,
They'll know, depending on the choice,
How much their ticks have grown.

One gives all hope the kiss of death.
His church is in the sticks
In place obscure (like Nazareth)
And won't gain any ticks.

One has a church that is well-known
For heroes of past days,
And so his line of ticks has grown
This vicar's hopes to raise.

One visited the old and sick
Who soon would be quite dead.
So this one did not get a tick.
"A waste of time," thought Fred.

Another wrote a long report,
"Church care for Old and Sick."
"Now that's real work," our Freddie thought
And gave this priest a tick.

Some mixed with folk who are the least
As all the Gospels teach
And tried like Chaucer's parish priest
To practise what they preach.

Some others took good care to mix
With folk who really matter,
And so their pile of Freddie's ticks
Steadily grew fatter.

Some priests seek not, nor win, renown,
Content their faith to share.
Some priests win fame in London town
Who church committees chair.

When prize day comes scout Fred will count
The ticks on each and all.
Some pile of ticks on high will mount
And some remain quite small.

Envoi
Thus Fred the scout has been around
With ticks for deeds and words.
Some clergy walk along the ground
While some fly high like birds.

These fly to pool of talent, then -
While others "Rev" remain, -
Hope to add "Very," "Right" or "Ven"
Or "Most" before their name.

The Archbishops' score, now well ahead,
So many ticks could boast
That as they'd had most ticks from Fred,
Their Rev. is labelled Most!

A problem recently has been accusations of abuse of vulnerable people, both with innocent being accused and guilty not being investigated. In 385AD Jerome contrasted both aspects (Letter XLV). As a result each parish has a safeguarding officer. This one is over-zealous in accusing the innocent. Jerome gave a list of false accusations: here we do the same in a more light-hearted way.

The Ballad of the Safe-Guarding Officer

I'm Safe-guarding Officer Claire
At St Bede by the Burn.
Vulnerable folk are my care.
Abuse is my concern.

I keenly make it my mission
To keep watch like a hawk.
If folk arouse my suspicion
They get a good, strong talk.

I thought I'd caught the predator.
The ladies of the choir
Were asked by th'Administrator,
"D'you feel, like me, on fire?"

Challenged, replied a predator,
"Heating falls to my lot.
The choir vestry radiator
Suddenly became too hot."

Cubs came to church with cub mistress.
This word caused me to rage.
I said to this vile seductress,
"These lads are under age."

I wrote to cub HQ complaining.
It made me feel a fool
When I read their note explaining
It's mistress as in school.

A young deacon who came here to train
First day stood far too near
Loud speaker controller Elaine.
Bad start to his career!

He, challenged, replied to my moan -
Elaine had stood near him
Only to fix the microphone
So everyone could hear him.

An old cleric, retired here, once shared
The Peace with young Beryl.
To hold her hand too long, he dared.
Oh! How great her peril!

He said, "My dear, I understand
Your fears about the Peace.:
Because of my arthritic hand
My grip I can't release."

At the Garden Club I heard folk say,
"The garden of th' Area Dean
Behind the hedge a fair display
Of naked ladies we've seen."

I arranged to have a photograph
To accuse a wicked Dean.
But at my expense folk had a laugh:
Pink flowers it showed - Nerine.

I heard of a vicar who in much lust
Emailed his secretary.
"Come tomorrow. Special massage. A must."
So I told the girl to be wary.

She replied, "No need for your scares.
About the email he'd sent.
It was about some special repairs
SPECIAL MESSAGE vicar had meant."

Th'Archdeacon caused great consternation
(Well, in my mind at least).
When upon his visitation
He kissed our lady priest.

Challenged, he said, "I'm indicating,
That though entitled, 'Ven'
And my job's administrating,
I'm just like other men."

I tried to have our bishop barred.
("Silly," I thought, "old fool").
He asked young Julie what she planned
To do when leaving school.

She, thinking he wanted to date her,
Said, "Go straight home from here."
Challenged, the bishop said later,
"I just meant - what career?"

Envoi
I'm safe-guarding officer Claire
At St Bede's by the Burn.
When I try to help folk in my care,
Things take a funny turn.

Curate and bishop accusing
With others in-between.
I've learnt that what seems abusing
May not be what they seem.

The University Safeguarding Officer

A dreadful case came to my care
In my line of duty.
A lady with soft, fluffy hair
Of unsullied beauty
Asserted that the College Dean
Abused her crowning joy.
Had stroked her hair, which aye had been
Untouched by man or boy.
This was, she claimed, sexual assault
In frenzy, mad and wild.
I accused him of this dreadful fault
Of beauty so defiled.
I said that he must surely pay
For this outburst of lust.
I asked him what he had to say
For PROSECUTE I must.

The Reply of the College Dean

From PROSECUTING please refrain.
This would cause great scandals.
I will this matter now explain -
Chapel's lit by candles.
This is for old tradition's sake
Though it's dim and stuffy.
This caused a very sad mistake
With her hair so fluffy.
In the Dean's comfy stall I dozed
Awhile and then awoke,
Saw fluffy head, my eyes half-closed,
And gave that head a stroke.
I thought I saw a pussy cat
A-creeping up on me.
Therefore in court I'll swear to that
As my Defendant's Plea.

Another person who made a mistake in
The Confession
I confess…
…in thought, word and deed.
I've brought my list of sins to read
…for absolution…
I need cleansing solution.
For renewal: Four cans of beer.
What's happened here?
Self-indulgence! Jar of best honey.
That sounds funny.
Six tins of beans.
Dunno what that means.
Two bottles of squash.
Oh dear! Oh gosh!
Three packets of tea.
I think I see.
Six slices of cake.
How I've made a mistake.
Packet of Bisto.
I've brought the wrong list! Oh!
Soup: Six tins.
And left my sins.
A nice lamb chop.
Behind in the shop.
For children, six lollies.
In one of Tesco's trolleys.
Three bars of soap.
I only hope.
Coffee: finely ground.
It won't be found.
Two packets of jelly.
By nosey old Nellie.
Six pots of yoghurt.
That list has my sins of thought.
Chocolate - a great big bar.
And my thoughts about Nell are
Packet of yeast.
Uncharitable, to say the least…
Well, that's the only sin I can confess
In spite of having made this mess!

The next four pages may have most meaning for those familiar with the Church of England. Page 116 refers to "Parties" in the church. One of the party differences had been the vesture of officiating clergy. A recent proposal would allow clergy to officiate without special vesture. This proposal inspired the following...

Puzzled Priest
A sonnet

When I was young and newly ordained
"Catholics," in their fine vestments arrayed,
- Stole, chasuble, maniple, alb - all claimed
To prove them legal, Canon Law should be made.
"Evangelical" voices said that this should
Not be the case and the church ought to say
That all wear cassock, surplice, scarf and hood.
The Canon was passed and all seemed okay.
Sixty years later and now I am old,
"Evangelicals," in suits now kitted,
Or t-shirts and jeans (so I am told)
Want a Canon to show they're permitted.
For a puzzled priest will some expert state
What these changes mean? (See Canon B8).

Part of this was published in the Church Times. It gives a relevance to the old story about the new vicar who wrote, "I intend to wear nothing in church to distinguish me from the congregation." The printer put a comma after church. We are not told whether this filled or emptied the church next Sunday.

To our dear Nanny Church
A sonnet for Swine Flu

In days long past a bold Spirit would fill
Mother church, by fearful folk surrounded,
If her suff'ring children were taken ill,
As pestilence, death, and plague abounded.
The clergy came without a fear of death,
Brought Sacrament and prayed by day or night.
No cream nor gloves for hands, no mask for breath.
Laid hands, anointed with the sacred rite.
But now - touch not the chalice: O beware
Of dangers lurking round the sacred feast.
Lest germs, not peace, we with each other share,
Shake not the hand of neighbour or of priest.
Dear Nanny trusts, faced with flu's infection,
Health and safety, not the Lord's protection.

This was written at the outbreak of swine flu. Its inclusion here is not
meant as a criticism of the necessary regulations imposed during the
more serious pandemic of Covid-19.

At the beginning of Covid-19 we were merely told not to shake hands. I
read out this light-hearted verse at "the Peace" -

Of handshakes now we must beware
Lest some awful germs we spread.
But "Peace" with each other may we share
With a kiss of peace instead?

128

The next two poems bring us to the world of academic theology. The first one shows the reluctance of some to believe that New Testament writings were written by those whose name they carry. St Paul's Letter to the Ephesians has suffered in this way.

The University Lecturer.

"The Letter called Paul to the Ephesians,"
said the Dean in a lecture one day.
"Modern scholars accept with good reasons
That who wrote it we cannot now say."

"Though differences there are stylistic,
At a more profound level we find
The deep thoughts of the things we call mystic
Here reflect Saint Paul's spirit and mind."

"He may have read Paul's works, so used Paul's name
For he'd absorbed Paul's thoughts as his own.
Perhaps their circle of friends was the same
Or the Apostle perhaps he had known."

One student remarked, "Considering all
These points you have made, they give reasons
For a New Idea, that the Apostle Paul
Himself wrote Paul to the Ephesians."

The Dean surprised, scratched at his head.
This New Idea perhaps was not wrong.
"Paul to the Ephesians," at last he said,
"May...just...possibly...to the Pauline Corpus belong."

One of the major theological influences in the second half of the twentieth century was Bultman's writings on the early church and expression of the Christian Faith for the modern world. Eventually some, whose propogation of the more radical elements caused controversy, rose to senior positions. The following was written after one broadcast address at Advent, in which the Visit of the Magi was said to be valuable without having gone through the formality of having actually happened. It is a parody of the Advent Hymn.

Hymn for a Liberal Bishop

Hark! An ancient voice is sounding
As each Christmastide we keep.
Words at Eastertide abounding
Lull the faithful ears to sleep.

Lecture notes now long forsaken
In some attic drawers decay.
His alone each year are taken
Out to see the light of day.

Radical was then that teaching
Stirring to the youthful ears,
Which again in modern preaching
At each Festival appears.

Nostalgic minds go then on trips
To a long-forgotten age,
When Bultmann's name was on all lips
And talk of Myths was all the rage.

Later writers may have altered
And their views are not the same.
His ideas have never faltered,
Firm as jelly they remain.

Whose this voice intensely pleading,
Fails to set our hearts aglow?
'Tis a liberal bishop reading
Lecture notes of long ago.

The New Model of Church Life
The Prelude

Shortage of cash: fewer Priests on the ground,
So a new model of Church life must be found,
"In this modern world," the Bishops decreed,
"A Manager-Priest groups of parishes need."
So the modern new incumbent uses a TRADITIONAL SONNET to
address his Flock:
"My dear people, – despite this well-known greeting,
I'll not make visits or want you to call,
TELEPHONE KEYPAD will be our meeting,
Cure of Souls, modern style, I explain now to all.
For times of H.C., press Number ONE,
To join our Church Choir Number TWO you must press,
THREE gives you Messy Church; that's lots of fun,
FOUR for Direction or Sins to Confess.
FIVE gives through Taped Messages, Pastoral Care,
Cleaning and flower rotas, they're Number SIX,
SEVEN'S for INFO on our big Parish Share,
EIGHT your Baptisms, Weddings, Funerals will fix,
When finally comes the great Day of Doom,
This we'll proclaim on our smart Parish Zoom."

Response by a Parishioner

I pressed Number FIVE for a Message of Care,
A voice said, "Press ONE if you're in despair,
Press TWO if you're worried about old Mum or Dad,
Or THREE if you've children who've gone to the bad,
FOUR if you're troubled by shortage of money,
FIVE if you're lonely and want something funny."
These options continued from SIX to NOUGHT,
According to need and the care that you sought.

Finale by the New Incumbent

Yes, in this way, all the Numbers on the main list,
We'll give further Options so nothing is missed.

We finish our section of Holy Laughter with another character, a representative of the opposition. This does not of course imply that all scientists are unbelievers. Some are well-known people of faith.

The Atheistic Scientist
A sonnet

This very learnèd scientific man
Was sure of many things we ought to know.
He showed us how the universe began
Some fifty million (billion?) years ago.
All mysteries of life on earth he'd solved
For which no written records can exist -
How birds from strange land animals evolved
Was shown by him who was an atheist.
"Why should we trust the Gospels?" asked this sage.
"For two thousand years ago they're dated.
From those old products of a bygone age
Our modern minds must be emancipated."
Billions of years ago can now be told:
Two thousand year old writings are too old.

End of Holy Laugher section.

The following pages have a mixture of themes, although the first one provides a link, being set in a churchyard.

For thirty-eight years, when responsible for the village churchyard, I could permit only straightforward inscriptions. We sometimes read in the press of disputes over this issue. Here my imagination has free rein, some based on last words; some may appear to have been written "aegro in corde"!

Apologies to Thomas Gray and his Elegy written in a Country Churchyard.

Elegy Written in a Suburban Churchyard

The streets light up as daylight starts to fail,
The roaring traffic fills southbound th'A3.
Commuters homeward plod by road and rail
And leave the world to darkness and to me.

Save that in each much overcrowded train,
In yon suburban home of well-bred taste,
Like moping owls folk to the moon complain -
Tonight's TV would be of time a waste.

Here in this Plot of Earth, neath built-up shade,
Where heaves the turf in many a moulding heap,
Strange folk, each one his own mistake who made,
Lie here. Oh read their epitaphs and weep.

Here lies Frau Schmidt
Who one summer night
On a visit to England
Drove on the right.

With parachute upon his back,
Dick jumped out, to save his skin:
But the parachute was a haversack
Which had the pilot's lunch within.

Journeys now past, here at home lies Ray
Who once went on a wild places holiday.
On the lofty terrain
Thin air affected his brain.
He mistook a big fuzzy bear
For his wife sweet and fair.
With his mind in a muddle
He attempted a quick cuddle.

Here lies a lovely girl called Mabel
Careless, though we loved her dearly.
She could not wait to read a label
Where EXTERNAL USE ONLY was written clearly.

Here lies Mad Major Mac, who in battle once said
(For the sake of a bet),
"I'll prove it's quite safe if I just raise my head
Above the parapet."
(The bet was paid, for sad was his fate,
Out of Mad Major Mac's estate.)

In your thoughts please remember
Dear Jack who loved Jill.
On the fifth of November
To give her a thrill
In his overcoat pocket,
Love's fire to represent,
Jack had placed a big rocket.
Too soon off it went.

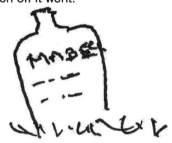

Jean, who lies here, was colour blind.
A group of mushrooms she did find
And on that tasty dish she dined.
At her inquest botanist said,
"Those 'mushrooms' were spotted bright green, blue and red."

Jacques sat in the train by a window.
The window was open wide.
As the train entered a tunnel,
"Look out!" his neighbour cried.
Jacques' English was very literal:
He mistook the words that were said.
He looked out of the open window
And literally lost his head.
His body lies here underground
But his head was never found.

Here lies speedy Sam now motionless,
Who did commit a grave mistake.
At sight of pretty maid in skimpy dress
His mind did a wrong direction take.
In wild confusion he with foot did press
Th'accelerator 'stead of brake.
Oh young men! learn from Sam's distress
When driving, thoughts of love forsake.
And ye, fair maids, let not your loveliness
Cause some poor swain to perish for your sake.

Here lies our wise cathedral dean,
An expert in the church's mystics.
In foreign gath'rings often seen,
Though with no talent for linguistics.
In a church group he went to share
A very special Kirchen fest,
Stayed at the home of pastor there.
Was welcomed as a special guest.
On the bathroom stand he found a flask
GIFT labelled in large letters red.
Grateful he was, nor stopped to ask
What these large letters really said.
"How kind," he thought, "of my good host
A gift to leave: I can say 'dank.'
To him I now propose a toast."
Then all within the flask he drank.

Beneath this stone lies dear friend Pat,
Found miles away in a home-made crater.
He was going up to his high-rise flat
In a powerful new elevator.
But when it had reached his floor at the top
Pat pressed START instead of STOP.
Having flown above earth dear Pat was laid
Here below with deep love and feeling.
(Th'insurance company have paid
For the big hole in the ceiling.)

Here lies at rest in deep Shalom
Good rabbi Ben from Israel.
How he came here, far from home
The following sad verses tell.
Driving from a garden centre
The rabbi had a great surprise.
About the busy road to enter -
Red lights flashed before his eyes.
POTS WON - he read th'information:
A game he'd entered just for fun.
He accelerated with elation,
Thinking of the prize he'd won.
His native language was Semetic,
With letters read from right to left.
Through this small mistake linguistic
Ben was of earthly life bereft.

Epilogue
They rest their heads upon this lap of earth,
These folk to fortune and to fame unknown.
Their epitaphs we read with silent mirth
But melancholy claims them for her own.

Reading of each mistake with tears and smile,
Dear reader, pray a solemn warning take.
Pause now and ponder thine own life awhile
Lest thou, like them, commit some grave mistake.

On these two pages the author expresses his incompetence with technology and computing.

Technology - the new Barbarism
A sonnet

Technology is a wonderful boon:
The most valuable form is I.T.
Communicate with the Man in the Moon,
With old friends across the wide sea.
Speak to each other at work by emails.
Hotels in Paris? - Push knob for info;
The doctor's machine has all your details,
Sat Nav will tell you the way you should go.
Technology is a terrible bane,
No time for books, only nonsense to share,
Irritate other travellers by train,
Cannot read Latin and deep thought is rare,
So I'll use my carrier pigeon instead:
At least I can eat them when they are dead.

The Non-Handy Man
An Ode in (perhaps not very good) French

Grand miracle de ma vie!
Chose incroyable!
Quand je coupe à la scie
Le bois sur la table.

Je veux faire nouveaux rayons,
De mon garage tous dignes:
Avec bien taillé crayon
Je marquee droite la ligne.

A la règle ferme je mesure
L'exact millimetre
Sur la planche nouvelle et dure
Ou la coupe doit être.

Oh! Si soigneux mon étude!
Car enfin je veux
Que chaque planche (exactitude!)
A la même longer.

Après des heures quand je vois
Rayons finis, je demande
(Miracle! Incroyable!) pourquoi
Trop petit est l'un
Et l'autre trop grand!

These two pages have verses inspired (if that's the right word) by the lockdown of 2020 / 21. Both the Lament and the Confusion are caused by folk not leaving the house.

Lockdown Lament
A sonnet by a burglar

I am what folk call a self-employed lad,
For I am a burglar: Bill is my name.
The tricks of my trade I learnt from my dad:
My well-paid career would cause him no shame.
When couples leave houses empty all day
I force open windows, doors I can smash.
Safes I can break in my own skilful way.
My wages were silver, jewels or cash.
No wages come now: folk all stay inside.
Through Covid-19 my life's not the same.
No house can I rob: they're all occupied.
Self-employed! - but compensation daren't claim.

With the lonely, unemployed, old and ill,
Oh! Please spare a thought for poor burglar Bill.

Lockdown Confusion
A sonnet by a cat

With this same family I now have been
For all my life so far - that's thirteen years.
And every year there is one thing I've seen
Which troubles me with worries and deep fears.
When the days grow long and the sun is bright
They leave our house, with bag and haversack.
I'm fed by friends, but left alone at night.
Anxious, I wonder - will my folk come back?
This year was strange, they did not go away
Though the sun shone brightly in the sky.
They did not leave our house one single day.
Puzzled I was, though pleased, and wondered why.
Careful, I listened, and "Lockdown" I heard
But did not know the meaning of that word.

"The Passing years" is a theme that links these two poems, although in different ways.

The Duchess's Dream
A sonnet

A duke who once lived a long time ago
Became a powerful force in the land.
To assert his might and repel his foe
He built a castle, big, firm and grand.
There were feasts and jousting with minstrels' song,
Soldiers and servants his will to obey.
"This castle of ours," he declared, "will belong
To our ducal line until the last day."
His wife said, "Last night I had a strange dream.
Peasants paid to come: ENTRY FEES I read.
Strange signs were shown: TOILETS, TEAS and ICE CREAMS.
Odd-clothed folk peered at my four-poster bed."
"You dream," said the Duke, proud smile on his face,
"Of what in real life could never take place."

This poem was written after a visit to a mediaeval castle with a group of tourists, paying our entrance fees, all in modern - some in odd - dress. I then wondered what the aristocratic mediaeval owner would have made of it all. This poem is the result, with its ironic ending.

Traces of Youth
A sonnet

It's mainly built-up now, with urban sights,
Houses and shops along a busy street.
Unending stream of cars, and traffic lights.
A supermarket, flats, car park, concrete.
Yet still is left a trace of rural scene.
A wooden barn, a tree of ancient years.
A broken fence, some patch of sodden green:
To the mind's age th'old rural scene appears.
She's in her nineties now, with hair turned gray
And yet her sudden smile, her eyes that gleam,
Her merry laugh roll the long years away:
The mind's eye sees a girl, nineteen
So in both urban sprawl and well-worn faces
Countryside and youth have left some traces.

This poem was written after driving into an area that became
increasingly more urban, yet with remnants of its rural past. This led on
to thinking of people whom I know in their later years and imaging their
appearance when young and finding some traces of youth.

In England I'm called an OAP.
Which does not sound too good to me.
In Germany things are much better.
We'll change the third and second letter.
There I'm called OPA. - that's not too bad.
It's a children's word for dear grandad.

143

The Saw Mill
A tragic ballad

On a saw mill once there worked two men,
Who worked hard all the day.
One's name was Jack, the other's Ben,
Very good friends were they.

Then while at work one fine spring morn
Jack gave sudden groan,
Because the saw machine had sawn
His hand off through the bone.

Ben sealed the hand in a plastic bag,
Drove Jack to A and E.
He'd written Jack's name upon the bag
For the surgeon there to see.

Ben went to the hospital next day
To ask about friend Jack.
The surgeon said he'ld be okay
For his hand had been sewn back.

The surgeon said, "Your action quick
I heartily commend.
That plastic bag has done the trick,
Tight sealed, it saved your friend."

In the next month one summer morn
Jack gave another groan.
Because the saw machine had sawn
His foot off through the bone.

Ben sealed the foot in a plastic bag,
Drove Jack to A and E.
He'd written Jack's name upon a tag,
For the surgeon there to see.

Ben went to the hospital next day
To ask about friend Jack.
The surgeon said he'd be okay:
His foot had been sewn back.

The surgeon said, "Your action quick
I heartily commend.
That plastic bag has done the trick:
Tight sealed, it saved your friend."

Then three months on, one autumn morn
Jack gave another groan,
Because the saw machine had sawn
His head off through the bone.

Ben sealed the head in a plastic bag,
Drove Jack to A and E.
He'd written Jack's name upon a tag
For the surgeon there to see.

He went to the hospital next day
To ask about Jack's head.
The surgeon said, "I have to say
That your friend Jack is dead."

Ben said, "I do not understand:
What happened to poor Jack?
For could you not, like foot and hand,
Have sewn his head right back?"

Envoi
The surgeon carefully replied,
"Alas! It was too late.
That plastic bag, tight sealed and tied,
Made Jack's head suffocate."

The Beautiful Blond
A light-hearted ballad

Now a beautiful blonde was Mary Jane
But she was not very bright.
For a week in Paris by aeroplane
Mary Jane had booked a flight.

Economy seat she could just afford:
'Twas shown on the boarding pass.
But when folk were called the 'plane now to board,
Mary Jane sat in first class.

The stewardess said, with a jealous look,
"I can see your little trick.
You grab the best seat though cheapest you book.
Off to economy! Quick!"

"As for tricks," beautiful blonde said with scorn,
"Your face is one I dare say.
My beauty is that with which I was born.
Now in this seat I shall stay."

A young pilot said, with smile on his face,
"Terribly sorry, my dear.
Through someone's mistake you're in the wrong place,
I'll escort you to the rear."

Said the beautiful blonde with all her charm
Which led that young man astray,
"Sweetie, I'm not doing anyone any harm,
So, darling, please let me stay."

An official came, in his file he brought
Copies of payment receipts,
Quoted figures to prove that Mary Jane ought
To accept a change of seats.

But Mary Jane said, "The figures you've shown
Are too hard for my poor brain.
The only figure I care for - my own!
In this seat I will remain."

They called the captain in consternation,
Hoping to find some way
To resolve this awkward situation
Of a girl resolved to stay.

The captain spoke to his team around him.
"I know just what to say.
This blonde, though a beautiful girl, is dim,
And soon will not want to stay."

The captain whispered in Mary Jane's ear.
At once she rose to her feet,
And hurried back, with a look of great fear,
To an economy seat.

The captain's team asked in admiration,
"Whatever words did you say
That solved this awkward situation
And made her not want to stay?"

Envoi
"That girl is not bright," the captain replied,
"So I told her to take great care,
For this 'plane into two parts will divide
Once we are in the air."

"The economy part to her chosen place,
To Paris city will go,
While the first class part a long route will take
To far-off Tokyo."

The Fisherman and the Tycoon
A thoughtful ballad

The fisherman sat on the beach in the sun,
And a happy man was he.
While his little boat, now his day's work was done,
Was anchored nearby at sea.

The tycoon had left his large yacht in the port,
And a busy man was he.
"I'll relax for a while on the beach," was his thought,
"To enjoy the sunlit sea."

Then he saw the fisherman half asleep
But thought this sight wasn't funny.
"You should be working," he said, "to earn your keep,
Then you would have loads of money."

The fisherman said, "Enough money I make.
All that I need I can buy.
To work longer hours, for more money's sake -
I can see no reason why."

Like a shrewd businessman the tycoon replied,
"Your money soon will have grown.
After meeting your needs, put money aside
And soon two boats you will own."

The fisherman said, "With this cash in the bank
And two fishing boats at sea,
This doubled income, to be perfectly frank,
What help would it be to me?"

"You could buy more and more until you possess
Your own fishing fleet out at sea,"
The tycoon explained. "At last you'll progress,
A millionaire then to be."

The fisherman pondered deeply in thought,
Then he asked the tycoon to say
What he as a millionaire then ought
To do with himself all day.

Envoi
"With no struggle and strain just to make ends meet,
Life," th'other said, "would be fun.
You could sit on the beach, put up your feet,
Enjoy the summer sun."

"Without all this trouble and huge fleet of ships,
Enjoying the sun as you say,"
The fisherman said, with a smile on his lips,
"Is what I'm doing today."

A piece of prose that may appeal to those who receive glowing Christmas newsletters from friends and relations.

Jennifer's Jottings
Christmas
Hullo everyone!

Here we are again after a wonderful and eventful year - and one so excitedly different from usual!

Jeremy and I had a most original holiday - a week's B&B in Scunthorpe. Lincolnshire (I think it is - you know my geography!) is so bracing and open, a change from our cosy Surrey Hills (and change is the *raison d'être* of holidays). Plus some industrial archaeology, as our B&B faced a disused steelworks. To think that we would have endured our usual scorching heat in the Caribbean if Jeremy had not been made redundant as Chief Executive of Mega Bank! Thank you credit crunch!

We have had a completely new kitchen fitted! All thanks to mummy and the insurance company. It was an exciting day. The fire brigade man assured us that elderly ladies like mummy often do silly things such as forgetting to turn off the gas fire under the chip pan. If they had been ten minutes later the whole house would have been burnt. How lucky we are! Thank you, mummy dear!

Joline has widened her experience by acquiring a new boyfriend - a real Cockney lad with big earrings, so different from her usual boring public school types. He is something in the medical export business (very hush, hush) and gave Joline a parcel to carry on her gap year. There was some misunderstanding at Customs, but eventually a lovely man from the British Embassy sorted it out. A newspaper is paying Joline for her article, "Six months in a Saudi Arabian prison." With such a career who cares what the headmistress of St Monica's wrote about her A-level results? I cannot stand sarcasm and LIFE matters more than exam results.

We also have a new car! A dear little bijou Ford (one careful owner, 4785 miles). Now that the children are fleeing the nest this is more suitable than our big BMW, which had a dramatic death. Jocelyn is an adventurous lad, so after getting his provisional licence he drove in his cavalier style at 90mph along the High Street at midnight. I have now complained to the council about the lamp-post in that spot. Jocelyn - athletic rugger player that he is - managed to leap out before the BMW burst into flames. The insurance company people were not so helpful over this incident. Stuffy old fogies - were they never young?

Now that Jeremy is spending more time at home with me, I am glad to have some activities curtailed. What a relief that Fyona Whatshername was elected WI president instead of me!

So that's our year - what does next year hold? "Pastures new" perhaps, for Jeremy has been head-hunted: post of Chief Night Caretaker at the above-mentioned disused steelworks in Scunthorpe. You can't keep a good man down!

With the season's greetings to everyone from
Jennifer and the four Js (including Jagger the Labrador)

Ode from the Author to a Critical Lady

While these verses I wrote and collected
Much time I had to spend.
"House dusting" one said, "You've neglected."
So this failure I here must defend.

The Defence

I have as vicar officiated
At many funerals year by year.
On each death certificate is stated
The CAUSE OF DEATH in letters clear,

Some died with a STROKE though HYPERTENSION
Or PNEUMONIA the "Old Men's Friend."
Some had diseases we must not mention
Whose lifestyle caused their sad end.

Some folk had gone out in the freezing cold.
HYPOTHERMIA is written there.
Others were simply just terribly old:
Certificates OLD AGE declare.

One fell from his horse when out for a ride.
MULTIPLE INJURIES it read.
For one star-crossed lover 'twas suicide.
Death's cause was SHOT HIMSELF IN THE HEAD.

One became OBESE for he loved to dine:
His wife - DISEASE GASTRONOMIC.
Another who drank excessively wine
Died from POISON ALCOHOLIC.

So many CAUSES OF DEATH have there been
And to record the truth we must,
Yet in all my life I have never seen
THE CAUSE OF DEATH was HOUSEHOLD DUST.

Finale

As we come to the close of the book, we finish with a poem for the close of the day.

Kanga's Nachtlied
with apologies to Goethe

Über allen Gipfeln ist Roo.
From peak to peak he leaps with glee.
But Kanga calls, "O where are you?
Eyeore and Piglet had their tea,
Th'animals all have gone to rest.
Christopher Robin's gone to bed too.
Wol is awake but in his nest.
Warte nur, balde ruhest du."

"If Memory
be Truth..."

Poems
Hymns
Meditative Verse
with Notes

Stanley Hemming-Clark